MERGER MANIA

MERGER MANIA

ARBITRAGE:
Wall Street's Best Kept Money-making Secret

IVAN F. BOESKY

Edited by Jeffrey Madrick

Holt, Rinehart and Winston / New York

Published by Holt, Rinehart and Winston,
383 Madison Avenue, New York, New York 10017.
Published simultaneously in Canada by Holt, Rinehart
and Winston of Canada, Limited.

Library of Congress Cataloging in Publication Data
Boesky, Ivan F.
Merger mania.
1. Arbitrage.   2. Investments.   3. Hedging (Finance)
4. Consolidation and merger of corporations.
I. Madrick, Jeffrey.   II. Title.
HG4521.B565 1985   332.64'5   84-25193
ISBN 0-03-002602-4

First Edition

Designer: Victoria Hartman
Printed in the United States of America
1 3 5 7 9 10 8 6 4 2

ISBN 0-03-002602-4

Dedication

My father, my mentor, William H. Boesky (1900–1964), of beloved memory, whose courage brought him to these shores from his native Ykaterinoslav, Russia, in the year 1912. My life has been profoundly influenced by my father's spirit and strong commitment to the well-being of humanity, and by his emphasis on learning as the most important means to justice, mercy, and righteousness. His life remains an example of returning to the community the benefits he had received through the exercise of God-given talents.

With this inspiration I write this book for all who wish to learn of my specialty, that they may be inspired to believe that confidence in one's self and determination can allow one to become whatever one may dream. May those who read my book gain some understanding of the opportunity which exists uniquely in this great land.

Contents

Acknowledgments

Portions of this book are based on lectures given during a course I have taught for several years at the Graduate School of Business Administration at New York University. I would like to thank certain people who participated in these lectures. They include Jim Fogelson, Ted Forstmann, Steve Fraidin, Carl Icahn, Steve Oppenheim, Harry Schick, and the late Arthur Dixon.

I also would like to thank Steve Fraidin, Arthur Fleischer, Jr., Victor Friedman, and Steve Oppenheim for their help in reviewing this book for legal and accounting accuracy.

In addition, I would like to thank Therese McNally for her research effort, as well as Nancy Hollander and Seema Boesky for their contribution in coordinating the review of the book. I also would like to acknowledge the help of Jane Dresner, Harold Tucker, and other members of my staff (past and present) for their assistance. I also want to express my appreciation to Steve Wasserman of Holt, Rinehart and Winston/New Republic Books for his help in preparing the book for publication.

My heartfelt recognition of the encouragement, guidance, and caring provided through the years by my mother, Helen Boesky. Finally, my affectionate appreciation to my wife, Seema, and children William, Marianne, Theodore, and Jonathan who have provided the security of a warm and loving home, which has helped to give me the strength to meet the challenges of each day.

Foreword

The United States can boast of the greatest securities markets in the world because of the competitive interaction of traders, investors, and market makers. In search of a profit, these market participants assure a fair and true price for all buyers and sellers. In turn, our corporations are able to raise capital in the most efficient and least costly ways. But there are no easy ways to make money in the securities markets.

I doubt that there are more exaggerated stories told about any single financial activity than there are about risk arbitrage. Of the many functions that contribute to a fair, liquid, and efficient marketplace, risk arbitrage is probably the least well understood. In classic arbitrage, the arbitrageur's function is to equate the price of a commodity in one market to the price available in another market. He buys goods, commodities, or securities that are selling too cheaply in one market, and then sells them in a marketplace where the price is higher. The price may rise in the market where it was cheap and may fall in the market where it was expensive until the price is the same in both.

Risk arbitrage has its roots in classic arbitrage. The arbitrageur bids for announced takeover targets that he believes are undervalued in the marketplace relative to their ultimate value. But in so doing, he provides liquidity to the marketplace. Unlike classic arbitrage, he also takes on risk that the rest of the market will not accept. For instance, a retired couple who has held 300 shares of Getty Oil for twenty years will welcome an opportunity to sell shares at a large profit and not worry whether Texaco will ultimately buy the company. So too will many a sophisticated financial institution. The arbitrageur can better assess the risks and rewards, and he knows more about limiting the risks.

This book is intended to explain an activity that has been hidden from public view for no good reason. Undue profits are not made; there are no esoteric tricks that enable arbitrageurs to outwit the system. All arbitrageurs lose money on occasion. The skilled arbitrageur will win often enough to make a profit, but profit opportunities exist only because risk arbitrage serves an important market function.

The role of risk arbitrage has been central to the functioning of the securities markets for many decades now. It has given Wall Street some of its most illustrious leaders: Gus Levy of Goldman Sachs, Harry Cohen of L. F. Rothschild, Salim B. Lewis of Bear Stearns, and Bunny Lasker of Lasker, Stone and Stern. Among Wall Street professionals, it is one of the most respected of crafts. I believe it should be more fully understood by the general public. This book is dedicated to ending the tall tales about risk arbitrage.

INTRODUCTION

Merger activity has always ebbed and flowed, and the characteristics of each new wave are different in significant ways. Chronically low stock prices and relentless inflation were the principal causes of the corporate mergers of the 1970s. It was cheaper to buy than to build from scratch. But in 1982, the economic environment had changed and the number of mergers fell sharply. A bull market in stocks in the summer of that year pushed prices of attractive companies higher, and inflation had subsided. Many Wall Street analysts believed that the extraordinary merger wave of the 1970s, which produced the largest business combinations ever, had ended. At the least, it looked as if merger activity was in for a long hiatus.

The vitality of the merger mania that began by the end of 1983 was thus unexpected and unprecedented. In 1984, new records were set for the size of acquisitions. A new movement had begun, but this time the strategy of corporate acquirers had changed. Rather than reaching into new areas of business, corporations were intent on sticking to what they knew best. They now bought companies in their own or closely related fields. So-called conglomerization was no longer fashionable. New strategies and financial techniques were devised. The leveraged buy-out became a popular method of acquiring companies. Stock and debentures frequently were used as a means of payment; in the 1970s, it had usually been cash.

Throughout each successive merger wave, the basic role of the risk arbitrageur remained the same: to make a living by investing in companies being acquired. At first glance, the arbitrageur's job may seem simple. But once a merger proposal or takeover bid is announced, the arbitrageur must assess all the factors that will determine the outcome. There is always considerable risk that a deal will not go through. Of course, that possibility is why there are opportunities to profit; why, to be precise, there is usually a difference between the price being offered and the price at which the target company's stock is being traded. That difference is called the spread.

An arbitrageur must consider many issues that are often bewildering, while pursuing his profitable prize. Many novice arbitrageurs have been right about the outcome of a proposed merger, only to lose money on the deal. A delay in completing a merger, for example, can significantly alter the potenial return. The terms of a deal might change if the overall economy changes. The action of an antitrust agency can suddenly end a merger. The trained arbitrageur uses a variety of financial techniques to limit these risks wherever possible. He continually balances risk and reward. These tools of the trade do not change, nor do the basic questions about the viability of a merger. Much will depend on the economic soundness of the merger, the financial muscle of an unfriendly acquirer, the current attitude of the antitrust authorities, the determination and psychological grit of the participants, and the economic environment of the current merger wave.

This book is designed to provide the fundamental framework on which future arbitrageurs can build their talent and expertise. Its objectives are primarily twofold: first, to be clear and accurate in a field that seldom has been written about, and then only obscurely; and second, to cover all the important aspects of arbitrage without all the technical detail. With this book alone, one could not be an accomplished arbitrageur, just as an athletic person could not race in a World Cup downhill competition after reading one book on how to ski. Nevertheless, a good arbitrageur could not practice his craft without knowing everything in this book. Every deal has aspects that raise new problems or require the judgment of professionals in other fields—lawyers, accountants, public-relations experts, proxy solicitors. Moreover, the technical factors that affect arbitrage—the law, federal regulations, accounting rules—are changing all the time. But this book is the first comprehensive presentation of the fundamental theory of merger arbitrage.

Few mergers in my experience have been as exciting as Texaco's last-minute purchase of Getty Oil Company in early 1984. Here was a situation that called on all the talents of the arbitrageur and presented the most basic and subtle issues an arbitrageur must face. The deal had its genesis in the restless ambition of Gordon Getty, J. Paul Getty's son and heir. He was a man who had always stood in the giant shadow of his prodigious and difficult father. I felt that Gordon Getty may now have wanted something out of his father's company. Through the Sarah C. Getty Trust, he already controlled 40 percent of it. As one of the beneficiaries, his annual income from dividends was about $30 million. Although the son sat on the board of directors, he could not control the company's policies. Did he want to? It never became clear. Perhaps Gordon Getty never precisely knew.

It turned out that it did not matter. A rumbling of discontent in the breast of a man in Getty's position was enough to set off a chain of events that he himself might not be able to control. Making a judgment about Gordon Getty's motivation was the main task of the arbitrageur in this deal.

Because his stake gave him a position of enormous power, assessing Getty's objectives and tenacity would be crucial. Because I believed the son may have wanted to get back at the father, I ultimately invested quite heavily in this deal. Some background is necessary to understand why I did so.

In mid-1983, Getty Oil stock was selling in the sixties. Earlier in the year it had been trading in the fifties and the total value of the company at that price was about $5 billion. It was rich in domestic reserves of oil. The company would not by definition become a target for risk arbitrage until a bid for the company surfaced late in 1983. But few companies looked more intriguing as a possible takeover candidate. Well before the bid was made, events occurred that indicated a bid was likely. The analysis of these events was much like the analysis an arbitrageur would undertake once a deal was underway.

The most important factor that favored a takeover at Getty Oil was the overall economic environment. The price of oil had fallen during the worldwide recession of 1982, but a vigorous recovery had begun in the United States. The Organization of Petroleum Exporting Countries (OPEC) finally had agreed to hold the line on oil prices, after having previously lowered them. By the fall of 1983, oil prices were beginning to steady.

In addition, there already was takeover activity among oil companies. And for good reason: to find and develop oil would probably cost more than to obtain it by simply taking over a publicly traded company with plentiful reserves. T. Boone Pickens of Mesa Petroleum Company was making all of corporate America aware by his takeover attempts that oil companies could be bought for low stock prices. Most Wall Street oil analysts agreed, right or wrong, that such stock prices did not reflect the true value of these companies. Getty Oil shares, for example, were worth nearly three times what they were selling for in 1983, according to one widely quoted estimate by Herold and Company. That fact could not have escaped Gordon Getty's attention.

There was another factor, the sort that always catches the restless eye of the arbitrageur. C. Lansing Hays, the other man besides Gordon whom his father had entrusted to run the huge Sarah C. Getty Trust, had died in the spring of 1982. Now only Gordon controlled the 40-percent block. If Gordon Getty could align himself with the J. Paul Getty Museum, which owned about 12 percent of Getty Oil, together they would have majority control. As soon as an arbitrageur sees that a relative handful of individuals can control a company, his interest is automatically aroused. In this case, only two individuals had to agree: Gordon Getty and Harold Williams, a former chairman of the Securities and Exchange Commission, who headed the museum.

At my firm, I have a "special situations" portfolio for just such investments. I analyzed Getty Oil's reserves and concluded that they were worth even more than Herold had estimated. Coupled with the other facts outlined above, Getty was an attractive investment. I started buying.

In October 1983, the first hard evidence that a takeover bid was possible surfaced. A so-called standstill agreement signed between Getty and the oil company's management was publicly announced. It read like a for-sale sign. While the agreement called for an end to hostilities, it served instead to confirm to outsiders that the two sides had been warring.

What apparently had happened was that Gordon Getty had been pressuring Getty Oil's managers to increase the value of the stock to shareholders. There were several ways to do this. The least controversial plan involved buying back some Getty shares in the open market. Other choices were to form a royalty trust or to search for a buyer outright. The company's management clearly did not want to accede to Getty's suggestions. Most of the alternatives would result in their losing control, and probably their jobs. They, in turn, sought to reduce Gordon Getty's grip.

The standstill agreement made all this clear. The company agreed not to issue new shares, which would have diluted the controlling interests of Gordon Getty and the museum. And it promised not to adopt anti-takeover measures. For their part, Getty and Williams on behalf of the museum agreed not to sell their shares to an outsider. Getty Oil's stock did not fall upon the news, as one would expect after a conventional standstill agreement. It actually rose several points. I was among the buyers. The standstill agreement was the proof that there were two warring factions. Even though the agreement was for a full year, odds were high that it would not last, that something—or someone—would give way.

When the standstill agreement was announced, Getty was trading in the seventies. It was not yet an arbitrage deal. Still, it made sense to analyze the potential risk and reward. If no takeover developed, Getty's stock probably would drop only 5 to 10 points. After such speculation, stock prices seldom fall all the way to their previous levels, which in Getty's case would have been only about 15 points anyway. But the possible gain if a takeover battle developed was much greater, perhaps 50 points or more. Most analyses placed the value of Getty, if liquidated, at $150 a share or more. Buying more Getty for my "special situations" portfolio made good sense.

The standstill agreement also called for the expansion of the board of directors from twelve to sixteen members, the additional members to be chosen by Gordon Getty and the museum. The new directors were announced a few weeks later; nothing made me more certain that a takeover battle would develop as the announcement of who the directors would be. Getty had named activists—in particular, Alfred Taubman, a real estate investor who had been instrumental in the massive sale of the Irvine Ranch; and Laurence Tisch, chairman of Loews Corporation, a renowned takeover specialist. I bought still more Getty shares on this news. The price was in the mid-seventies, but I still felt the rewards far outweighed the risks.

Within a few days of the announcement of the new board members, the standstill agreement collapsed. A relative of Gordon Getty challenged his position as sole trustee of the Sarah C. Getty Trust. To virtually everyone's surprise, Getty Oil's management joined the suit against Gordon Getty, asking that a "disinterested" party be appointed as co-trustee. Why join the suit after signing the standstill agreement? By later accounts, the board voted to do this after asking Gordon Getty to leave the room. Gordon Getty's advisers claimed this was a violation of the standstill agreement because the control of his position was being challenged. It looked now as if any chance of rapprochement between management and Gordon Getty no longer existed. Up to this point it was possible Getty and the museum could have been eventually mollified if Getty Oil bought back a large number of shares in the open market. This no longer seemed possible.

By now, Getty Oil was as close to a takeover contest as you could get without one's having been declared. One more final blow was dealt in early December. Gordon Getty and the museum entered into an agreement that gave each the right to buy the other's shares before they were sold to a third party. In other words, the two had banded together, and together, it will be recalled, they had more than 50 percent of Getty Oil. Experience indicates that majority control almost always wins, no matter what management tries to do. As if to impress this new union on Getty Oil, the museum and Gordon Getty acted jointly a few days later to change the bylaws of the company. Under the laws of Delaware, the state in which the company was incorporated, the majority owners were allowed to do this. What they did was to bar Getty Oil's management from taking any action against owners of 5 percent or more of the company without the support of fourteen of its sixteen directors. This was a direct attempt to block the suit challenging Gordon Getty's status as sole trustee.

Enter Hugh Liedtke, a consummate deal maker, who had built an oil company from scratch by organizing oil partnerships. As head of Pennzoil Company, Liedtke also had proved that he could buy companies. Pennzoil today is a thriving company. In the Getty turmoil, it is no surprise that Liedtke saw his chance. Pennzoil could not possibly afford to take over all of Getty, but Liedtke could exploit the dissension at the company and maybe get what he wanted for much less. A couple of days after Christmas, Pennzoil announced a partial-tender offer for Getty Oil. The company would buy 20 percent of the outstanding shares for $100 a share. At last, the Getty Oil machinations had resulted in a public bid.

Most arbitrageurs were caught by surprise, and they did not entirely like what they saw. Assuming that Gordon Getty would not tender, what is known as the blended value of the offer was about $88 a share. This is a common computation that arbitrageurs always make. If Pennzoil took 20 percent of the outstanding 48 percent (or 42 percent of the arbitrageur's holdings) not owned by Getty and the museum, one might be able to sell the remaining 58 percent of the shares for only $80. That was about the price at the time of the bid. The combined or blended value of all the shares then is $88.

The arbitrageur must always compare risk to potential reward. To me, the $88 offer did not represent a ceiling; I felt it really represented a floor. It was the least that I could expect to receive for my shares. If one was convinced, as I was, that another bidder would come in at a higher price, then one could buy shares for any price up to $88 without fear of taking a loss. I believed the potential for big gains was great, but an offer probably would have to exceed Liedtke's $100 a share.

Three factors favored a third-party bid. First, Getty Oil had no "natural" defenses against a takeover. The federal government, I believed, would almost certainly not object on antitrust grounds. Because the oil industry is so large, even a $10-billion merger would not create undue market concentration. Nor were there significant regulatory concerns.

Second, Getty Oil's management was acting very much as if it wanted to avoid falling into the hands of an unfriendly owner. It was fighting Gordon Getty vehemently. Hugh Liedtke could no doubt act like T. Boone Pickens, maybe not ultimately controlling the company, but very likely pushing it into the hands of an unfriendly buyer—even possibly Gordon Getty himself. Getty Oil's management had every incentive to hunt for what is now commonly known on Wall Street as a "white knight," a company that will bid higher for the target and is friendly to management.

Third, oil was once again in demand. While I did not believe a non-oil company would make a bid (current corporate philosophy was to stick to what you know best), there were several giant oil companies in dire need of reserves that had suffered major failures in recent searches for oil. In addition, oil prices were rising that winter, largely because of unusually cold weather across the nation.

However, there also were two major risks for an outside buyer. The first was the sheer size of the deal. To buy out all of Getty Oil would require as much as $8 billion, and perhaps several billion dollars more. Only a few companies could arrange that kind of financing.

The second major risk was Gordon Getty himself. Did Gordon Getty really want to run Getty Oil? Was his principal motive to maximize the value of the trust's shares?

He could perhaps forge a deal with Liedtke, who had already declared that he wanted to work with him. Gordon could then run the company without making a bid for the remaining shares.

Despite these risks, my conclusion was that the likelihood of another bid was very high. The Pennzoil bid would force other bidders to play their hand soon. Banks were flush with money then and had no difficulty making loans based on oil as a commodity. There were some potential acquirers around with a great deal of cash on hand. And they were hungry. As for Gordon Getty, I believed he ultimately would have to go for the highest offer. He was, after all, charged with guarding the interests of the entire Sarah C. Getty Trust, not just his own. The museum, whose interest was its endowment and not the oil business, undoubtedly would sell to the highest bidder.

Finally, my risk-reward analysis showed little potential loss. I regarded the $88 blended value, as previously noted, as a floor. The issue to be resolved was how much profit I was willing to forgo if I was wrong, not how much I might lose. The Pennzoil bid, I had concluded, was simply the bait that would bring the hungry hunters out sooner than anyone expected. I invested heavily in this deal.

After the New Year's weekend of 1984, Pennzoil and the Sarah C. Getty Trust announced an agreement that they would purchase all remaining shares for $110, plus an additional compensation for the sale of a Getty subsidiary. Gordon Getty would get to run his father's company; Liedtke would get his oil reserves. Most important, Getty Oil's management publicly agreed to the proposal. Liedtke had apparently pulled it off.

But it took Texaco only two days to jump into the act with a $125-per-share bid for the whole company. The agreement between Pennzoil and the Sarah C. Getty Trust no longer mattered; the higher bid would win. That was the final irony, and a key lesson for the arbitrageur in this deal. Pennzoil and Getty Oil's management neglected to sign their agreement before the deal was announced. The stipulation in that agreement that might have prevented the Texaco takeover by requiring the issuance of additional shares could not therefore be upheld. A signed agreement is de rigueur to the arbitrageur. It proved to be a colossal legal oversight. Because a definitive agreement was not made public—and I searched hard to find it—I bought shares even after the Pennzoil deal with Getty was announced. I knew there was still a door open for a higher bidder.

Before it was all over, Texaco would raise its bid another $3 a share to $128 in order to satisfy several dissenting Getty heirs and the Federal Trade Commission would have a look and require some adjustments. On February 3, the commission approved the Texaco bid. On February 13, Texaco bought all the shares tendered. On February 17, the merger was legally consummated.

The biggest merger in history to that date was very profitable to arbitrageurs. Other giant oil mergers were to follow, raising new opportunities for profit and causing much controversy within the federal government. These mergers too were ultimately allowed to proceed. The biggest of all time, a $13-billion acquisition of Gulf Oil, would take place in May largely at the provocation of T. Boone Pickens. There were many other deals, less spectacular but large, interesting, and profitable nonetheless. A new wave of mergers had clearly begun. Risk arbitrage was more exciting and lucrative than ever before. Every major financial house had its own arbitrageur. It was no longer an esoteric specialty practiced by a few secretive individuals. Arbitrage had arrived. It was as much a part of Wall Street as the mutual fund and the stock trader. And it deserved a book.

1
WHAT IS
RISK ARBITRAGE?

What is it that attracts an otherwise normal investment professional to arbitrage? The action, of course, can be fast, the hours taxing, the rewards ample, the risk substantial. But the main attraction to me, and I think to many of my colleagues, is that arbitrage is such a sensible investment practice. This may surprise most readers who are accustomed to hearing about the high risks, big profits and big losses, and freewheeling nature of risk arbitrage. That impression stems more from hearsay than reality.

In point of fact, traditional investment management never has made much sense. An analyst may fully understand a company he is following, may even be able to forecast its future earnings with unmatched precision. Does that mean he can forecast its future stock price with any precision at all? Of course not. Price-earnings multiples averaged as high as 25 or so in the heyday of stock trading in the 1960s. In the mid-seventies these multiples had fallen to 6 and 7. Any stock price is buffeted by sweeping market forces that are virtually impossible to predict with any reliability. These forces are often important: the growth rate of the economy, the course of interest rates, the international value of the dollar, the inflation rate, an overseas war, a Presidential election. They also can be distressingly unimportant: this week's change in money supply, the Federal Reserve Board's sale of securities, its reversal of that sale the next day.

Risk arbitrage, too, can be affected by unpredictable forces. But they are much less uncertain than those of traditional investment management.

What is risk arbitrage? It is the taking advantage of the disparity of value that exists between two different but related securities that are trading simultaneously in the same or different markets, or the disparity between the market price and the cash price being offered. The possibility for such an investment arises not only in corporate takeovers, but also in liquidations and other company reorganizations.

The essence of risk arbitrage is to understand and carefully measure the risk of an investment. It is also to limit that risk by certain kinds of market transactions. Hedging all possible risks is central to risk arbitrage. The danger of big swings in the overall stock market, for example, is relatively insignificant in merger arbitrage (now the predominant form of risk arbitrage) and frequently can be eliminated. What risks remain can be assigned reasonable probabilities.

Risk arbitrage is not gambling in any sense. Done properly, the odds of a risk arbitrage investment are with you, not against you. Traditional stock investing is much closer to gambling than is risk arbitrage. I remember following an international oil stock very closely as a young analyst. I knew everything there was to know about it; I could estimate quarterly earnings with extraordinary accuracy. What I could not predict was a political eruption in a Southeast Asian country. As a result, the stock price plummeted and I sought a less futile vocation. I lost a great deal of money and did not get it back until the company, Natomas, became the target of a takeover fourteen years later.

Because arbitrage is not at all like gambling, it is no accident that risk arbitrage has attracted some of the most respected of Wall Street's investment banking firms. Today, many of the best and most successful firms in the financial community have active arbitrage operations. Arbitrage has accounted for a significant—and growing—share of the profits of such firms as Goldman Sachs and Company, Salomon Brothers, Bear, Stearns and Company, and L. F. Rothschild, Unterberg, Towbin.

Few activities on Wall Street, or anywhere else for that matter, are as intrinsically entrepreneurial as risk arbitrage. Successful arbitrageurs are independent minded and willing to take risks. They generally have renounced the chance to live a more bureaucratic but perhaps less grueling life. There is a thrill in this sort of independence, a certain kind of excitement in putting oneself on the line all the time and trying to come up a winner. For example, few deals in the financial history of the United States put risk arbitrage more clearly on the map than the battle initiated by United Technologies Corporation, under the bold hand of Harry Gray, Jr., when it made an unfriendly tender offer for Babcock and Wilcox Company in 1977. The relatively smaller McDermott, an oil-rig manufacturer, bided its time, carefully assessing its position. It quietly bought up stock in Babcock. Rumors abounded. Arbitrageurs hung in. Soon, McDermott made a bid, and eventually it won. In that deal, arbitrageurs were the big winners. The thrill of that victory is one that I shall always remember.

Of course, there have been disappointments, deals that fell apart, losses that somehow had to be endured. But the first requirement of a good winner is to know how to lose. The arbitrageurs I know have dared to be defeated and still manage to be victorious in the future.

How can one learn to practice risk arbitrage? Any fundamental book about arbitrage will be a primer, a manual of the rules of the game. The practice of risk arbitrage itself is a craft that borders on an art. More precisely, it is the artful application of the tools at one's disposal. Much the same can be said of painting, acting, or writing. To practice arbitrage well, then, requires more than schooling and more than capital. There is the doing of it. Only by doing it can one build a sense of a deal, an instinct for the risks, the comprehensive knowledge of sources of valuable data, the tax consequences and the myriad alternatives, and a grasp of the pertinent federal and state laws.

Arbitrage is one of the fastest paced of investment activities. It is not enough to know the problems and potential rewards. One must be able to decide very quickly. Risk arbitrage resembles art in that it requires the careful development of knowledge and technique. It also resembles competitive sports or military strategy. Technique and knowledge are important, but one also must act decisively, often with imperfect knowledge under extreme pressure, and occasionally while under attack in the throes of a deal.

The outcome of an arbitrage investment will be known in a fairly short time. The result is unforgivingly black-and-white. There can be no excuses for failure, no institutional rhetoric to hide behind, no committee on which to shift responsibility, no politician or international conflict to blame. You are on the line and visible, especially to your Wall Street colleagues. Good arbitrageurs seem to like it that way. They represent, I think, the best of America's entrepreneurial spirit.

The roots of arbitrage are embedded in the nascent and budding currency markets of Western Europe. It is almost medieval in tradition, its best practitioners having to serve a long apprenticeship. It requires painstaking attention to detail. It has been successfully practiced by only a relative handful of professionals. To this day, that practitioner is usually called by the French appellation *arbitrageur*.

To understand the extant literature on classic arbitrage

would require a working facility with French and German. Only a few publications have been written in English and these are mostly out of date. A book on arbitrage published in England in 1910 begins, "The literature on the subject of the present book is remarkably meagre." That unfortunate fact is still true.

For such reasons, arbitrage has appeared esoteric to outsiders. There is, in fact, much less mystery to it than is commonly believed. Arbitrage is a basic trading function in any marketplace. Its practice is essential to the smooth running of an efficient financial market. The origin of the word says more about its true meaning than do more modern definitions. It is derived from the French word *arbitrer*, which means to judge or to estimate. The English word *arbitrate* also sheds light on the subject. *Arbitrate* means to settle the difference between. In the older style of turn-of-the-century texts, one author provides this definition: "The arbitrage compares prices of articles of merchandise dealt in on various markets in order to find out their difference."

Modern definitions have become more technical as worldwide markets have become more sophisticated. Webster's Eighth New Collegiate Dictionary defines arbitrage as the "simultaneous purchase and sale of the same or equivalent security in order to profit from price discrepancies." This form of arbitrage, which is called classic arbitrage, probably originated in international currency markets where, say, the British pound trading in London could be bought at a different price than the pound trading in Amsterdam. The arbitrageur buys the cheaper one and, simultaneously if possible, sells the dearer one, retaining the profit. The discrepancies in classic arbitrage are small and the risk is low or nonexistent. The primary requirements for success are speed and accuracy.

But the earliest definitions of arbitrage are better guides to the true nature and purpose of the practice. The goal of arbitrage is to equate precisely the values of the same or equivalent securities, products, or commodities in different markets. For a market to work well, buyers and sellers must be confident that prices are fairly set and that equivalent securities will sell for equal prices. In an international currency market that means that a British pound should sell for the same price both in Milan and New York. For securities, it means that the same stock trade in Paris should sell for the equivalent price on the New York Stock Exchange. Moreover, a change in price in one of these markets should signal a change in price in all markets.

Since the last century, a brisk arbitrage business has been conducted in shares traded on various stock exchanges. The shares of the copper company Rio Tinto-Zinc Corporation, South African Gold Mines, and the Suez Canal, for example, were traded on both the London Stock Exchange and the Paris Bourse. If Rio Tinto opened ½ point higher in Paris than its last trade in London, an arbitrage opportunity was created. The arbitrageur could buy Rio Tinto in London and sell in Paris. The London price would rise and the Paris price fall until they were equal, less transaction costs. The result is that a buyer or seller gets the fairest price available in the two markets. Securities arbitrage was quite common among U.S. exchanges in New York, Boston, Philadelphia, and Chicago around the turn of the century. Today, securities arbitrage is practiced among dozens of exchanges around the world. Speedy communication and the ability to trade quickly are still required today as they were a hundred years ago. But, of course, the nature and speed of those communications, as well as the sheer size and sophistication of world financial markets, have required a commensurate refinement in the practice of arbitrage.

As markets in international securities and currencies developed, arbitrageurs saw opportunities for using their ability to gather information about buyers and sellers. An arbitrageur, for example, might notice heavy selling of a currency in New York and, knowing of eager buyers in Zurich, he might buy the currency in New York in the afternoon with the expectation that he can sell the next day in Europe at a profit. Of course, he might be wrong. Thus risk is introduced—the arbitrageur takes some additional risk for the possibility of a bigger profit. But so also is liquidity added to the marketplace—the arbitrageur buys currency when most people are unwilling to do so. He himself is holding that stock, using his own capital, until he can sell the next morning. And he might take a loss. One writer, fifty years ago, appropriately labeled such transactions tendency arbitrage. The arbitrageur recognizes a tendency toward a different price level and, despite the risk, seeks to take advantage of it.

Over the years, arbitrage activities have embraced far more than stock and currency trading. Convertible securities offer opportunities for arbitrage between convertible stock or bonds and the underlying security. Other areas include rights offerings, which are issued by corporations to existing shareholders and give them the right to buy new shares at a specific price; spin-offs and liquidations; and stubs, which are rights to future shares or earnings.

What is now called risk arbitrage has its origins in America in two historical developments, according to arbitrage specialist Guy Wyser-Pratte of Prudential-Bache. The first was the reorganization of major railroads in the late 1930s. Many of these lines suffered bankruptcies in the Depression years and issued new securities in exchange for the old in order to reorganize financially. The arbitrageur could buy the old securities and sell the new ones in "when-issued" markets, retaining the spread as a profit. The second development was the Public Utility Holding Company Act of 1935, which forced utilities to divest themselves of many of their subsidiaries. A discrepancy in price would ensue between the value of the new securities and the value of the parent company. Many arbitrage opportunities developed in these markets. But there were risks: the reorganization might not occur or the terms may have changed. Such arbitrage was therefore termed risk arbitrage.

Our main subject is mergers and acquisitions arbitrage. In the past two decades, it has come to be the dominant form of all risk arbitrage. When two companies announce a merger or one company announces a bid for another (whether it be friendly or hostile), a risk-arbitrage opportunity is created. A discrepancy generally develops between the value of the securities being offered (or the cash price) and the price of the target company's stock. That discrepancy exists because the deal ultimately may not be consummated and because its consummation, even under the best of circumstances, will take time. Time, to all investors, means money. The arbitrageur must weigh the risks and determine whether the potential reward is sufficient. Speed and the ability to trade are again important requirements in successful merger arbitrage. But what is termed deal analysis is the principal element required for successful merger arbitrage.

Merger arbitrage, one of the several types of risk arbitrage, is not merely buying a takeover target if you think an acquisition will be completed. In merger arbitrage's most basic form, risks are always being hedged by using many different types of transactions and securities. Merger arbitrage is not guessing correctly whether or not a merger will go through. Many amateur investors have been right about the outcome of a deal and have still lost money. There are many other factors involved, including the final value of the deal, its timing, and the cost of money. Merger arbitrage is not a one-decision investment. It is an ongoing process: prices fluctuate, the economy changes, government actions are taken, stock is always being bought and sold. Merger arbitrage is not a part-time activity. It requires constant vigilance.

Observers have come to think of modern merger arbitrage as only a distant cousin to classic arbitrage. No doubt the risks are greater, as are the potential rewards. But the basic similarities between the two are striking. Like classic arbitrage, merger arbitrage's ultimate effect is to equate values in the marketplace. In this case, the arbitrageur may bid up the price of the acquired company to a value that he believes through experience and analysis will prevail. As with tendency arbitrage, the arbitrageur also provides liquidity to the marketplace. He is typically buying from those who do not want to bear the risk of waiting to see if a deal will be consummated. These investors may not have the capital to hold on to their positions or they may simply be satisfied with the profit already made. They are not able to analyze a deal as well as the experienced arbitrageur and do not have his trading abilities.

The key conceptual point to be made is that the arbitrageur takes risk and provides liquidity in ways very similar to an international-securities arbitrageur who sells shares he bought in New York to buyers in Amsterdam. When an announcement for a takeover is made, the arbitrageur may be willing to pay more for a stock than a financial institution believes it is worth. He will buy the stock, usually at a sizable profit to the financial institution. In turn, he expects to sell that stock to the acquiring company at a profit. The arbitrageur can attach a higher value to the stock because he is more knowledgeable about the risks, has unique analytical skills, can trade more effectively, has considerable experience, and can act more quickly. He is forcing up the price of the target company closer to what is in his opinion its realistic value. He is equating prices and values of related securities—the historical and classic arbitrage function.

Merger arbitrage came to full fruition in the 1960s. Mergers had been common enough before then, of course. In

England, there was a wave of hostile takeover activity beginning in the early 1950s. Some of that, in fact, washed over the United States in the 1950s and mid-1960s. But the spate of mergers that was to sweep over the American financial community in the late 1960s was in many ways unprecedented. Unusually high stock prices dramatically set the stage, as did liberal accounting rules. Many corporations found they could acquire companies with an exchange of their high-priced stock and raise their earnings per share virtually automatically. As with all such movements, there was some logic to it. At that time, many of the best minds in business management believed there were synergistic benefits in combining two companies. It was the age of conglomerization. Such companies as IT&T and Gulf and Western Industries were flying high. The volume of mergers tripled between the mid-1960s and the late 1960s. The opportunities for arbitrageurs were excellent. A great deal of money was made.

When stock prices came down, so did merger activity, at least temporarily. But in the early 1970s, a new merger wave began. This time the stage was set by runaway inflation and the energy crisis. Cash, not stock, became the most overvalued of financial commodities. Stock prices fell so low that most companies were selling at bargain prices. It became much cheaper to buy than to build. Cash tenders were widespread, and if a company did not choose to be acquired, then major corporations did not hesitate to go ahead with a tender offer anyway. (Cash tender offers will be discussed in Chapter 6.) Hostile mergers became common. Total merger activity set new records, rising from about $12 billion in 1971 to $44 billion in 1979, and $82 billion in 1981 to more than $100 billion in 1984. Again, arbitrage opportunities abounded. Indeed, arbitrageurs have played a central role in the two merger waves of the past quarter century. They will continue to do so.

Summary

Merger arbitrage, the predominant form of risk arbitrage today, is not simply an investment in takeover targets. Its roots lie in the risk-limiting hedging techniques of classic arbitrage. In classic arbitrage, an investor buys the same or the equivalent product or commodity in one market and sells it simultaneously for a slightly higher price in another market. Over the years, arbitrage expanded to riskier practices. But always the same basic objective applied: risks are limited. In merger arbitrage, risks can be carefully assessed and restricted through financial techniques in important ways. Potential profits must be properly calculated and weighed against these risks. The function of merger arbitrage, as with all arbitrage, is to make securities markets work more efficiently.

2
THE MERGER-
ARBITRAGE TRANSACTION

A merger occurs when two separate companies combine into one. Depending on legal, tax, and accounting considerations, a merger can take three forms.

1. Two companies can create an entirely new legal and corporate entity.

2. One company can be absorbed into the operations of another.

3. One company can become a division or wholly owned subsidiary of another.

An arbitrage opportunity is created during a merger when the acquiring company offers more for the company to be acquired than its current selling price.

The Basic Merger Transaction

The arbitrageur must always ask himself whether the potential profit is worth the risk. For instance, if Company A offers stock worth $10 a share for Company B, which is trading at $7.50 a share, will the potential profit of $2.50 a share be worth the risks? These risks include the timing, ultimate value, and likelihood of completion of the merger. The discrepancy between stock prices—in this case, $2.50— is called the spread.

But while a typical investor may see an opportunity to buy Company B at $7.50 and wait until the merger is completed to receive his $10, the arbitrageur sees something subtly but importantly different. He sees a chance to undertake the basic arbitrage transaction. As with classic arbitrage, that transaction is the simultaneous purchase of one security and the sale of another that can be exchanged for it. In this case, the arbitrageur will buy Company B at $7.50 and sell short Company A at $10. This transaction eliminates any risk due to fluctuations in the market prices of Company A or Company B. For example, if Company A's price fell to $9.50, the arbitrageur would have earned only $2. But by implementing the above transaction, the $2.50 spread is assured. Locking in the spread is at the heart of all arbitrage.

Let's make the example more realistic. Suppose that Company A proposes to merge with Company B for an even exchange of stock: one share of Company A for one share of Company B. Company A is selling for $30 a share on the day of the merger announcement. Company B is selling for $20 a share. The price of Company B immediately rises to $25 a share (before trading is suspended temporarily, as is typical with such an announcement). The $5 spread is the arbitrageur's potential investment profit. It exists only because the shares of Company B cannot immediately be exchanged for the shares of Company A. The spread may shift as the likelihood of the merger grows, the time until it is consummated shortens, or the market prices of the respective companies change.

The arbitrageur seeks to lock in the spread as his profit, and that is the purpose of the basic merger-arbitrage transaction. If the arbitrageur buys Company B for $25, a risk is taken that the price of Company A could fall below $30 before the merger is legally consummated. The arbitrageur, therefore, will not only buy Company B but also sell short an equivalent number of shares of Company A in order to lock in the spread of $5. This spread is assured no matter what happens to the subsequent price of the two companies. Selling securities short is the sale of securities that are borrowed, not owned. The securities must be returned to the lender either when the arbitrageur receives the shares in the merger or when they are purchased in the open market.

> ARBITRAGE TRANSACTION: Buy one share of Company
> B @ $25
> Sell short one share of Company A @ $30

Let's say that over the course of the deal the price of Company A falls to $27. The deal is then consummated with Company A at that price. Company B is therefore worth only $27 as well. But the arbitrageur still retains a spread of $5. The transactions when the deal closes will look as follows:

> TRANSACTION: Sell one share of Company B @ $27
> Cost = $25, Profit = $2
> Buy one share of Company A to cover short position
> @ $27
> Short Sale Proceeds = $30, Profit = $3
> Total Profit (Spread) = $5

The $5 spread also will be retained if the price of Company A rises. If the deal is finally made when Company A equals, say, $34, the following transaction will have been undertaken by the arbitrageur.

TRANSACTION: Sell one share of Company B @ $34
Cost = $25, Profit = $9
Buy one share of Company A to cover short position
@ $34
Short Sale Proceeds = $30, Loss = $4
Total Profit (Spread) = $5

In this way, arbitrageurs hope to eliminate the vagaries of unpredictable bull and bear markets, economic surprises, changes in investment fashion, and the myriad factors that generally require so much attention in conventional investing.

But there seldom is a one-for-one exchange of stock in the real world. More typically, Company A would not be selling close to the price it would like to offer for Company B. For example, let's assume that Company A's stock is selling for $24 but it still wants to offer about $30 of its stock for Company B. It would have to exchange 1.25 shares for every share of Company B to equal the $30 value. The merger-arbitrage transaction, then, would not be simply to buy one share of B and sell short one share of A. The arbitrageur would have to sell short the equivalent number of shares he would be receiving in exchange for one share of Company B. In other words, he would sell short 1.25 shares of Company A for every share he bought of Company B. This would lock in his spread.

The Workout Value

Unfortunately, mergers can get still more complex. They often involve an exchange not only of shares but also of other kinds of securities and cash. As a result, the combination or package of securities being offered is frequently intricate. Determining what is called the workout value of an offer is the first and most important step in the arbitrage process.

The following examples illustrate several basic kinds of merger transactions. Determining workout values often involves pricing new securities or evaluating securities whose value will fluctuate with interest rates. No amount of examples can cover the many possible variations. The offer can involve debt securities, preferred stock, different classes of stock, warrants, and convertible securities, many of which may be newly issued. But the following real-life examples cover the key variations. Appendix A includes proxies and other information on each of the following examples.

Stock for Stock

Aetna Life and Casualty Company and Geosource:

TERMS: 1 share of Geosource = 1.25 shares of Aetna

A stock-for-stock merger is the most basic transaction and typically the easiest in which to determine the workout value. In the spring of 1982, Aetna Life and Casualty and Geosource announced a mutual agreement to merge. Aetna, the insurance company, was determined to diversify. It had chosen thermal energy, Geosource's business, as a good way to begin.

The terms of the deal were simple. For every share of Geosource, the shareholder would receive 1.25 shares of Aetna. At the time of the announcement, Aetna's share price was $44. Geosource was trading at $32. After the announcement, Geosource's shares rose swiftly to $50. Computing the workout value shows us why.

Workout value = Aetna's share price ($44) × 1.25 = $55

If the merger were completed the next day, a share of Geosource would be worth $55, or $5 more than the closing price that day. The basic transaction was a classic example of the merger-arbitrage transaction. For every share of Geosource bought long, the arbitrageur would sell short 1.25 shares of Aetna—the precise equivalent of the number of Aetna shares to be received. The spread is then locked in. The importance of locking in the spread is particularly well emphasized by this example. Over the course of the merger, Aetna's price dropped to $36 and, correspondingly, Geosource's price fell to about $43. But the arbitrageur suffered no loss as a result. Let us see why. Assume Geosource can be bought for $50 a share.

TRANSACTION: Buy 1 share of Geosource @ $50
Sell short 1.25 shares of Aetna @ $55
Spread = $5

On completion of deal:

1 share of Aetna = $36
1 share of Geosource's = 1.25 × Aetna's price = $45
Loss on Geosource's long position = $5
Gain on Aetna's short position = original selling price ($55) − current price ($45) = $10
Net gain on deal = $5 per share, or same as original spread

Cash and Stock

The Coca-Cola Company and Columbia Pictures Industries:

TERMS: 1 share of Columbia Pictures =
        (1) $32.625 plus additional cash equal to 1.2
        × the average closing price of Coca-Cola
        (on the fifteen trading days prior to the ef-
        fective date of the merger)
                    OR
        (2) 1.2 shares of Coca-Cola plus additional
        shares equal to $32.625 at the time of the
        merger (computed by dividing $32.625 by
        the average market price as defined above)

Here's a fairly complicated transaction. For a variety of reasons, Coca-Cola chose to offer either cash or stock to Columbia shareholders, although the amount of cash available would not be sufficient to redeem all the shares. The arbitrageur would make a decision as to whether to take stock or cash partly based on tax considerations (these will be more fully discussed later in the book). The point to be made here is that the two choices were substantially identical in value on the day of the merger. The Columbia shareholder received 1.2 shares of Coca-Cola and the equivalent in Coke shares of $32.625 (based on the average market price for the prior fifteen days), or $32.625 in cash plus additional cash worth 1.2 shares of Coke (also based on the average market price).

What is the basic arbitrage transaction in this deal? The objective is to lock in the spread on that part of the deal that can fluctuate. The $32.625 in cash (or the stock equivalent of that much cash in the second alternative) will remain fixed over the duration of the proceedings. There is no need to lock in this amount. But the portion of the deal that is tied to 1.2 times the value of Coke shares can change. Therefore, the arbitrageur would sell short 1.2 shares of Coke for every share of Columbia purchased. Let us run through the calculation. Coca-Cola shares equal $33 and Columbia Pictures shares equal $58.

> TRANSACTION: Buy 1 share of Columbia Pictures @ $58
> Sell short 1.2 shares of Cola-Cola @ $33
> Value of package at current Coca-Cola price = $72.225
> Spread = $14.225

The arbitrageur would undertake this transaction whether he chose cash or stock for Columbia shares. The $32.625 is fixed and will be received in cash as the equivalent stock whether the price of Coke rises or falls. The value of the package that is contingent on the Coke share price can be hedged by selling those shares short. This, of course, is the basic merger-arbitrage transaction. Examining the final value of the package demonstrates how the spread was locked in:

> Arbitrageur receives cash
> Coca-Cola = $30
> Cash received = $32.625
> Additional cash received = 1.2 × $30 = $36
> Total value of 1 share of Columbia Pictures on completion of merger = $68.625
>
> Cost to purchase 1 share = $58
> Gain on sale of Columbia = $10.625
> Gain on short sale of 1.2 Coke = $3.60 (short sale price [$40] − cover price [$36])
>
> Total gain = $14.225, or same as original spread

Two-Step Merger: Cash and Debt

In the early 1980s, so-called two-step transactions became common. An acquiring company could gain effective control of the target by merely tendering an offer for a majority of the shares—in other words, more than 50 percent. This was the first step. As the second step, the remainder of the shares could be exchanged for a security rather than for cash. The United States Steel Corporation's takeover of the Marathon Oil Company is a good illustration. It also is a case where a new debt security was issued.

Early in 1981, U.S. Steel made a successful cash tender offer for 51 percent of the shares of Marathon Oil. It paid $125 per share for 30 million shares. A month later, U.S. Steel offered a new 12½-percent guaranteed note with a face value of $100 due in 1994 for the remaining shares of Marathon.

FIRST STEP: Cash tender for 51 percent of shares at $125 a share

SECOND STEP: $100 principal amount of new 12½-percent guaranteed notes due 1994 for each Marathon share

The arbitrageur's principal task is to assess the value of the new notes—a traditional task of investment banking. Comparable securities in quality and maturity are examined that already are trading in the marketplace. Judgments must be made about the comparative values of these securities. Time is also a factor; interest rates in general might shift before the new securities begin to trade. The arbitrageur must decide whether it is desirable to bear this interest-rate risk (there are methods to hedge, if imperfectly, in the interest-rate futures market). If a sufficient spread exists between the arbitrageur's valuation of the new notes and the price of Marathon stock, a long position in Marathon can be taken. But unlike conventional merger arbitrage, a hedged position cannot be taken until the new securities begin to trade. In this case, the notes would begin trading on a when-issued basis, in a few weeks. At that point, the arbitrageur can sell short the notes against a long position in Marathon stock.

As with the basic merger-arbitrage transaction, the spread would be locked in no matter how the price of Marathon or the new notes fluctuates.

Stock for Cash or Combination of Securities
ConAgra and Peavey Company:

> TERMS: One share of Peavey =
> (1) $30 in cash
>
> OR
>
> (2) A package of newly issued convertible pre-ferred stock plus common stock of Con-Agra

Here is a particularly complex deal. The workout value is difficult to compute. And it turns out that there is no perfect hedge available to the arbitrageur. In this case, the company offers cash for only 30 percent of all the outstanding shares of the target company. The remaining 70 percent of the shares would be exchanged for a package of convertible preferred stock, newly created for this purpose, and common shares equal to a stated amount of cash. The complicating factor is that a so-called collar, a common arbitrage term, is placed around the number of shares of common stock that can be exchanged. This protects the acquiring company, but it also makes hedging the transaction virtually impossible.

If the arbitrageur chooses to receive cash from ConAgra, he could get as little as $9 a share—30 percent of the total $30. The remaining $21 worth, or 70 percent, will be the package of securities. The terms of the securities package are as follows:

(1) 0.172 shares of newly issued ConAgra $2.50 cumulative convertible preferred stock

PLUS

(2) The number of ConAgra common shares equivalent to $25.70 in cash, determined by dividing $25.70 by the base-period stock price (defined as the average of the daily highs and lows for a fifteen-day period). A maximum and minimum number of shares is stipulated.

The arbitrageur can at least hedge against the convertible security—the new cumulative convertible preferred stock. This can be accomplished if a when-issued market develops, as in the U.S. Steel–Marathon Oil example. But the arbitrageur also may hedge against the possibility that the ConAgra stock price will fall to a level that could cause a loss because there is a maximum on the number of shares to be exchanged.

What complicates this package is the insertion of the minimum and maximum number of common shares to be exchanged no matter at what price level ConAgra is trading when the deal is completed. When the exchange is based on an average price, it is not uncommon to find such collars in a deal. The acquiring company intends to pay out shares that are equivalent to a cash price. But they also want to protect themselves if their share price moves much higher or much lower over the period that it takes to effect the deal.

The objective of the arbitrageur is to guarantee the value

of the securities package regardless of what price the shares trade at. How is this accomplished? Unfortunately, it seldom can be accomplished at an attractive spread. The most conservative strategy is to short the minimum number of shares that will be offered, according to the collar stipulations. In the case of this deal, the minimum is 1.035 ConAgra shares. No matter how high the price of ConAgra runs, the investor will get at least 1.035 shares. Therefore, if the arbitrageur shorts this amount, he will never be left with fewer shares to cover the short position. If he sold short more than the 1.035, a risk is taken of a loss on the short sales. The problem is that by shorting, the arbitrageur may have to settle for a smaller spread. More typically, arbitrageurs will analyze the price fluctuation of the stock as well as the prospect for sudden changes, and short differing amounts of the stock at different prices. At other times, the arbitrageur will not hedge at all until the averaging period (on which the share formula is based) begins. In this case, the price is based on the average of the highs and lows of the preceding fifteen days. The arbitrageur can short sell one fifteenth of the position each day to hedge the outcome very closely.

One other variable in the ConAgra-Peavey merger must be taken into account. An arbitrageur may know beforehand that he will opt for cash. Therefore, in this deal he will have to hedge only 70 percent of the package—the proportion that is not guaranteed in cash.

The sections of the offering document for each of these deals is included in Appendix A. The reader would do well to search these documents for the pertinent information summarized above. It is good practice to learn the formal language of these documents and to be familiar with the location of important information.

Summary

The basic merger-arbitrage transaction limits an important risk of merger arbitrage. Hedging limits risk, usually termed market risk, which arises when the share price of the acquirer or target company fluctuates while the merger is underway. Such fluctuations would otherwise change the terms of the deal and ultimately the rate of return available to arbitrageurs.

3
RETURN ON
INVESTMENT

The arbitrageur's quantitative analysis is not complete once the workout value is computed. The workout value, in fact, is only the first step in the ultimate computation for the arbitrageur: the return on investment. For the arbitrageur, determining the return on investment is similar to the businessman's capital-investment calculations.

A prime consideration in determining the return on investment is the length of time it will take the merger to be legally consummated. Time is money to the arbitrageur. When capital is put up for an investment, the opportunity to earn at least a bank's interest is given up.

A second consideration is the amount of capital being put up. The arbitrageur will borrow to invest in securities. The amount that can be borrowed is affected by government and stock-exchange margin and short-sale rules and by the arbitrageur's credit. Whether or not, and to what extent, profits can be taxed can greatly affect the size of the return of the arbitrageur's investment. Mergers where securities are exchanged are usually tax free. Cash tenders are generally taxable. In addition, each arbitrageur usually will have his own personal or corporate tax considerations to take into account.

There are five elements of the return-on-capital calculation to be considered.

1. Terms of the deal—workout value
2. Timing
3. Cost of money
4. Capital invested
5. Tax liability

The Return-on-Capital Calculation

The basic calculation is to determine the potential profit as a percent of the amount invested less financing costs. The return is then figured on an annual basis, according to the length of time the investment is tied up.

Let's return to our first example. Company A offered $30 for Company B trading at $25. Let's assume that the arbitrageur can borrow 50 percent of his investment on both long position and short sales, and that the cost of interest is 12 percent. The arbitrageur buys 100 shares of Company B for $25 and sells short 100 shares of Company A for $30.

TRANSACTION: Buy 100 shares of Company B @ $25
= $2,500
Sell short 100 shares of Company A @
$30 = $3,000

The arbitrageur believes it is likely that the merger will be completed in three months. The return-on-capital calculation is as follows:

1. The terms of the deal are an even exchange of one share for another share. The workout value at the current price of Company A is simply $30. The arbitrageur can lock in a

spread of $5 a share by selling Company A short and buying Company B, thus having a profit of $500.

2. If the deal is completed in three months, capital would be tied up for one fourth of the year, or at one fourth of the annual interest rate. To determine the annual return from the investment, we multiply by four.

3. The cost to borrow funds is 12 percent. Over three months, that would come to a finance charge of 3 percent.

4. The arbitrageur must put up 50 percent of the investment in capital. That is $2,750.

5. The exchange of securities qualifies as a tax-free gain.

Summary: The profit earned if the deal goes through is $500. The finance charge over three months is $82.50 (3 percent of $2,750). So the net profit is $417.50 on an investment of $2,750, or 15.2 percent. The annual return on capital is about 60 percent. The arbitrageur believes there is a high probability that the merger will go through, and even if it does not, the loss will be no more than a few dollars a share. Very likely, the arbitrageur will make the investment.

The Real World

When we leave the world of textbook examples, the rate-of-return calculation becomes more complex.

The timing of a merger can change if the pieces do not all fall into place smoothly. The arbitrageur must keep track of those separate pieces carefully.

The amount the arbitrageur can borrow will also depend on many factors. There are various government regulations that must be respected. In the end, it is often the banks, which of course provide the loans, that will determine how much and at what cost the arbitrageur can borrow.

Taxes also can be an intricate problem. Different arbitrageurs may have different liabilities, and certain kinds of transactions can be arranged to reduce tax liabilities.

Timing

No estimate of potential return on capital can be made without a good idea about when the proposed merger will become effective. Only then will the arbitrageur be able to exchange securities and realize a profit. There are many factors that can unexpectedly prolong a merger. Adverse rulings by government regulatory agencies can delay a merger for months. Under the Hart-Scott-Rodino Antitrust Improvements Act of 1976, mergers must be submitted to a federal antitrust agency for review and companies must be found to comply with the Clayton and Sherman Antitrust Acts. Court proceedings also can delay the consummation of a merger, especially if rounds of appeals follow. The Securities and Exchange Commission also might create delays by not approving proxy material as quickly as expected.

Most deals, however, proceed along a predictable series of steps. Of these, five are most important in determining when and whether a merger will be consummated.

1. A preliminary agreement, which is an agreement in principle to merge, is announced. Preliminary terms are set, comprehensive analysis and audits of the respective companies are undertaken, and government processing is begun.

2. The merger proposal is filed with the government antitrust agencies, which have the right to raise objections within thirty days.

3. A definitive agreement to merge is signed by the two parties. This signing is the most important of the steps. The definitive agreement sets the final terms and other criteria of the merger. Most companies that reach this stage will not back out of a merger.

4. The appropriate company or companies submits formal proxy material to the Securities and Exchange Commission. This proxy material will set a date for the shareholders' meeting. At that meeting, approval by shareholders is usually required. This also is a key step in the process.

5. A request for a tax ruling may be filed with the Internal Revenue Service. Many mergers are contingent on such a ruling. In complex transactions, it will take longer than customary. The sooner a filing for a tax ruling is made the better. When the arbitrageur knows the date a request for ruling was filed, a reasonable estimate can be made as to when that ruling will be made.

The experienced arbitrageur generally will have a good sense of how long each of these steps will take. He will follow closely the progress of each step, eager for announcements about the key steps and alert for any sign that something may go wrong. The procedure and the expected length of time for each step is clearly illustrated in the chart on page 42.

Financing an Arbitrage Position:
Margin Requirements and Net Capital Rules

For the professional arbitrageur, the return on capital can be effectively enhanced through the use of leverage, which requires that the arbitrageur put up a percentage of the value of the stock bought. There are two sets of rules that determine how much cash or capital an arbitrageur must have on hand in order to undertake transactions. The first broad set of rules are the margin requirements that fall under Regulations T and U of the Federal Reserve Board and as they are interpreted by the New York Stock Exchange, the National Association of Securities Dealers, and other ex-

Anatomy of a Deal
Common Chain of Events, with Average Time Periods

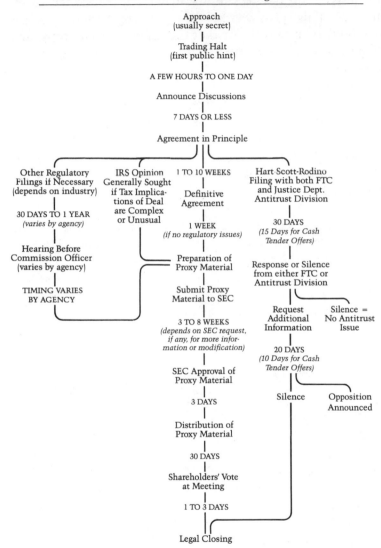

Approach
(usually secret)

Trading Halt
(first public hint)

A FEW HOURS TO ONE DAY

Announce Discussions

7 DAYS OR LESS

Agreement in Principle

| Other Regulatory Filings if Necessary (depends on industry) | IRS Opinion Generally Sought if Tax Implications of Deal are Complex or Unusual | 1 TO 10 WEEKS | Hart-Scott-Rodino Filing with both FTC and Justice Dept. Antitrust Division |

30 DAYS TO 1 YEAR
(varies by agency)

Definitive
Agreement

30 DAYS
(15 Days for Cash Tender Offers)

Hearing Before
Commission Officer
(varies by agency)

1 WEEK
(if no regulatory issues)

TIMING VARIES
BY AGENCY

Preparation of
Proxy Material

Response or Silence
from either FTC or
Antitrust Division

Submit Proxy
Material to SEC

Request
Additional
Information

Silence =
No Antitrust
Issue

3 TO 8 WEEKS
(depends on SEC request, if any, for more information or modification)

20 DAYS
(10 Days for Cash Tender Offers)

SEC Approval of
Proxy Material

3 DAYS

Silence

Opposition
Announced

Distribution of
Proxy Material

30 DAYS

Shareholders' Vote
at Meeting

1 TO 3 DAYS

Legal Closing

Source: Argus Research Corporation/Neil R. Feldman

changes. The basic margin requirement for both individual investors and registered broker-dealers is 50 percent of the value of the stock purchased. The margin requirements for securities sold short are generally 50 percent of the proceeds. The margin rules for options are more complicated. For example, the purchase of a call gives the buyer the right to acquire shares at an assigned price.

The "naked" sale of a call—selling a call without owning the underlying stock—would require a margin of 30 percent of the underlying market value plus an additional charge to the extent it is *in the money.*

There are some exceptions to the basic margin requirements. When the conditions precedent to a merger being completed have been met, for example, the New York Stock Exchange will consider the transaction bona fide and the securities can be carried on lower margin. In cases where a broker-dealer is also a market maker in a stock, margins can be lowered.

More complicated than margin requirements are the net-capital rules of the Securities and Exchange Commission. The conceptual basis of these rules is that securities firms must have a minimum amount of capital on hand against every holding in case the market value of these holdings falls. To arrive at the amount of capital required, a so-called haircut is applied to securities. The haircut will be least for securities of little risk such as Treasury bills, but will be significantly higher for corporate shares and options. Among securities firms, the specialist usually will be entitled to the most liberal requirements; the full-service broker who deals with the public will have to meet the most conservative requirements. Arbitrage firms sometimes fall in between, as brokers that deal for themselves, although many are part of larger firms that deal with the public.

It can take an experienced accountant hours to assess the capital requirements of a firm's arbitrage positions. But in the most general terms, the haircut for an arbitrageur's positions is 30 percent of all the long or all the short, whichever position is greater. Arbitrage firms also can choose an alternative means to calculate haircuts. In this case, the haircut comes to 15 percent of the long position, plus 30 percent of the shorts to the extent they exceed 25 percent of the long position. A firm that is long $1 million of stock must hold $150,000 in capital against this position. If the firm also is short the equivalent of $750,000 in stock, it must meet an additional haircut requirement equal to 30 percent of the $500,000 above the 25 percent (or $250,000) of the long position. That comes to another $150,000. Options present a particularly complex set of problems for determining haircuts.

The efficient use of leverage is critical to an arbitrageur's rate of return. The arbitrageur's relationship with the banks that supply the credit is important. The back-office operation of any arbitrage firm is responsible for servicing this function. In Wall Street accounting and billing functions were historically relegated to back-office status. That has changed over the years. For arbitrage firms the back office is particularly important.

Taxes

One of the most important factors affecting the arbitrageur's rate of return, and of course the investment decision itself, is the extent to which gains on arbitrage investments can be taxed. Unfortunately, tax liability is seldom simple to calculate.

There are two distinct tax issues that must be considered. First is the taxable nature of the merger or acquisition itself. Second is the tax status of the arbitrageur. Most mergers and acquisitions that involve an exchange of stock and securities are structured to meet Internal Revenue Service requirements that will make the exchange tax-free. Cash tender offers and the use of cash as part of an exchange will generally result, in whole or in part, in a taxable transaction to the shareholder. These gains, in turn, may be taxed as dividends, capital gains (long- or short-term depending on the owner's holding period), or a combination of these. Such calculations can become quite complex. Moreover, not all exchange offers involving only stock and securities qualify for tax-free treatment.

Inherent in the basic merger-arbitrage transaction is an important tax advantage. The securities of the acquiring company and the company to be acquired are, in general, not "substantially identical" until the merger has been approved by shareholders and remaining obstacles have been eliminated to the point that the respective market values of the stocks substantially reflect the proposed transaction. When an arbitrageur buys the shares of the company to be acquired long and sells the acquiring company short, the resulting gain on the long investment should the deal go through is capital gain. Any loss on the short position can be used to offset short-term capital gains.

In some cases, depending upon the length of time the long position has been owned, the capital gain is considered long-term, but gains on short sales are always short-term. There is no such advantage in tender offers. The gains from such offerings can be taxed as dividends or short-term capital gains. Whether the shareholder or arbitrageur is taxable as an individual or as a corporation must be taken into account in calculating potential returns on an arbitrage investment. Some arbitrage operations are set up as corporations largely to take advantage of the 85-percent corporate-dividends-received deduction (6.9 percent effective tax rate), though the benefit of the deduction may be reduced to the extent the long position is debt financed.

Tax Implications of the
Basic Merger-Arbitrage Transaction

There is an important tax advantage in the basic merger-arbitrage transaction. The arbitrageur typically buys the target company long and sells the acquiring company short. Ideally, the value of the target will rise, creating a gain on the long position. Often, the value of the acquiring company will fall, as discussed in Chapter 2. The short position will be at a loss. Prior to the approval of the merger by shareholders (and after approval has been given where remaining contingencies exist and the market price of the stocks does not substantially reflect the proposed merger), target- and acquiring-company stock will generally be treated as not substantially identical. If the two stocks are treated as not substantially identical, any loss on the short position will be short-term capital loss, and the long position, where desirable, can be retained until it qualifies as a long-term gain. With increasing scrutiny of merger arbitrage by the Internal Revenue Service, this procedure is best undertaken only with the advice of competent tax counsel. But it is significant in determining appropriate arbitrage strategies.

Tax-Free Exchanges

There are seven basic types of corporate reorganizations under the Internal Revenue Code. The first three (together with statutory variations) are the most important and will be discussed here.

Type A Reorganization

The Type A reorganization is generally the most common and most flexible of the tax-free reorganizations. It is essentially a statutory merger or consolidation in which the acquiring company absorbs the company acquired, or a third corporation is formed from the two former entities. Stock (common or preferred, voting or nonvoting) is exchanged for stock.

The great advantage of the Type A reorganization is that a minimum of only 50 percent in value of the consideration paid, according to Internal Revenue Service guidelines, must be in the form of stock (the "continuity of interest" requirement for qualification as a tax-free reorganization). The remaining 50 percent can consist of cash, warrants, or debt securities. In such cases, the stock-for-stock exchange is tax-free to the shareholders. The exchange of stock for assets may not be.

Type B Reorganization

A Type B reorganization is least flexible, and the methods of consideration are limited. To qualify for tax-free treatment under the Type B reorganization, the acquiring company must exchange solely its own voting stock (or the voting stock of its parent but not a combination of both) for stock of the acquired company. Immediately after the acquisition, the acquiring company must have "control" of the acquired company—i.e., own stock possessing at least 80 percent of the total combined voting power plus at least 80 percent of the total number of shares of all other classes of stock. (The stock exchanged by the acquiring company can be voting preferred stock.)

Type C Reorganization

The Type C reorganization is probably the least common type of merger. For legal reasons, a company may find itself unable to undertake a statutory merger. It buys outright the assets of the acquired corporation. To qualify as a tax-free exchange, the acquiring company must purchase "substantially all" of the target company's assets for stock. The remainder can be purchased for any other form of consideration.

In addition, the acquired company must distribute the stock, securities, and other properties it receives, as well as its other properties, in pursuance of the plan of reorganization. Experienced tax counsel is necessary to make such decisions.

"Triangular" Type A Reorganizations

"Triangular" statutory tax-free mergers may also be consummated where permitted by applicable state law. These transactions involve a target company, a controlled subsidiary, and a "controlling" company, the parent of the controlled subsidiary. In a forward triangular merger, the target company merges directly into the controlled subsidiary and the stock of the parent company is given as consideration for the acquisition. This transaction is treated as a tax-free reorganization if "substantially all" the properties of the target company are acquired by the controlled subsidiary. The merger would have satisfied the Type A reorganization tests had the target company been merged directly into the parent and if no stock of the subsidiary is used.

Similarly, the controlled subsidiary may merge into the target company (which is the surviving company) and the shareholders of the target company exchange their stock for voting stock of the parent (a reverse triangular merger). The reverse triangular merger qualifies as a tax-free reorganization if the surviving corporation holds "substantially all" of the properties of both target and subsidiary after the transaction and if, in the transaction, former shareholders of the target exchange stock constituting control of target for voting stock of the parent.

Step Transactions

A company that has acquired an interest in another corporation several months before with cash may not be precluded, under appropriate circumstances, from acquiring the remainder of the corporation under a Type B or Type C reorganization. If the two steps in this transaction are actually part of a plan to acquire the company, the Internal Revenue Service will generally take the position that it is a "step transaction" and consider it for tax purposes as one integrated transaction. But if the steps in acquiring a company are truly separate—usually meaning that sufficient time has elapsed between steps—they are considered independent transactions. The second step in the acquisition may then be treated as a Type B or Type C reorganization, if the particular qualifications have been met.

Target Rate of Return

When an arbitrageur makes an investment, he also must consider his portfolio of other arbitrage investments. He may have most of his capital, and borrowing capacity, tied up in other deals. Or the rewards for a given measure of risk might be greater for other deals. By the same token, the current opportunity might be so appealing that he will sell other positions to raise more available capital.

Some analysts talk about a target rate of return for the arbitrageur. That is, if the rate of return on a deal exceeds a certain level, say, 40 percent, the arbitrageur should invest. In my experience, there is much fuzzy thinking about the target rate of return. It is not the same as the probability student's expected value, at least as the target rate is customarily discussed.

The target rate of return should represent a rate that is high enough to compensate for the possibility that some deals will not go through and some losses will be suffered. The target return must take into consideration the possibility of losses. In the example cited on page 50, we might calculate the expectation that the deal will go through at 85 percent. In a friendly deal with few antitrust problems, an 85-percent probability of completion is realistic. The expected annual rate of return of 60.7 percent is then multiplied by the probability of consummation.

$$0.85 \times 60.7\% = 51.6\%$$

But we also must allow for the possibility of losses. Let us say that the loss also would equal 60.7 percent of the investment if the deal fell through. We deduce this by assuming at what price we can eventually sell out. The probability of that is 15 percent.

$$0.15 \times 60.7\% = 9.1\%$$
$$\text{Expected return: } 51.6\% - 9.1\% = 42.5\%$$

We must deduct the expected loss from the gain. Our probability-adjusted expected return, then, is only 42.5 percent. Arbitrageurs develop a target rate of return for themselves. But, again, that benchmark must take into account the probability of losses in the portfolio as well.

Summary

The arbitrageur must constantly reassess the rate of return as conditions change. The timing of the deal especially will shift. As each step is met along the way, the arbitrageur will become more confident about the deal and when it will be completed. Suddenly, the signing of the definitive agreement may be delayed or the tax ruling might not come through. The rate of return is significantly affected.

Some arbitrageurs will have access to more capital than others. Tax issues also will be different for different investors. But the essential elements of calculating the rate of return will remain unchanged.

4
TO INVEST OR NOT TO INVEST

Now that we have completed the purely computational side of arbitrage, we must grapple with the more subjective factors of judgment that affect the decision to invest. The arbitrageur must determine whether the proposed deal will go through, when, and at what prices. At this stage, he must be fluent in the special language of the accountant, the lawyer, and the financial analyst. Mastery of these vocabularies means that the arbitrageur must be a financial linguist. He also must be something of a psychologist.

A planned merger can fall through for a number of reasons:

1. The Justice Department or Federal Trade Commission may raise antitrust objections.

2. The shareholders may dissent.

3. Another company may bid higher.

4. Managements may come to insurmountable differences.

5. The target company may mount an unbreachable defense.

Similarly, a merger may be delayed or the terms of a deal may be altered for a number of reasons:

1. The economic environment may shift.
2. Management may discover unanticipated problems in the company to be acquired.
3. Commodity prices may fluctuate.
4. Legal action may result in delays.

How to Determine Whether the Merger Will Be Consummated

There are no simple formulas to determine whether a merger will be completed. Thus, good judgment plays a greater role than technical competence and subjective analysis outweighs risk calculation. The arbitrageur will explore diligently—and as quickly as is feasible—all aspects that might affect the outcome of the deal. Every merger also will provide new problems that will test not only the arbitrageur's skills and experience, but also his powers of observation and ability to apply those skills creatively.

The basic questions that the arbitrageur must ask in analyzing the prospects for any deal are the following:

Does the Merger Make Business Sense?

Mergers must be based on solid financial and economic principles. The business combination should result in a stronger business entity. In some cases, the strengths of one company should compensate for the weaknesses of another. In other cases, two similar companies may merge and the resulting company's larger size will allow it to compete more effectively in its market. In the 1960s, the economic rationale for many mergers was the application of better and more aggressive management by the acquiring company to the assets and businesses of the acquired company. In the

1970s, companies often were interested in buying assets or plants and equipment that were, in effect, selling more cheaply on the stock market than they would cost to replace.

A key tool in determining the economic sense of the merger is the pro forma balance sheet and income statement that will result. Such pro forma financial statements are generally included in the proxy material, but an arbitrageur will usually do the accounting analysis independently. The proxy material usually will not be ready for weeks, perhaps months, after the deal is initiated.

There are two acceptable methods of accounting for business combinations. The accounting rules established by the profession's rule-making organization, the Financial Accounting Standards Board, specify precisely which method is used under different circumstances. Knowing which method applies is important because they significantly affect the assets, liabilities, and earnings of the merged companies.

The first, known as the purchase method, is usually applied to acquisitions made for cash. The acquired company is recorded on the acquiring company's books as if it was an asset, such as a piece of equipment or a factory. The assets and liabilities of the acquired company are recorded at their fair values, not at historical book values. If the cost of the acquisition exceeds the fair value of the assets less the liabilities, a new asset is created called goodwill. Goodwill must be amortized and is a reduction to earnings.

The second method is called the pooling of interests method. This can be applied only where the rules specifically allow it, usually for exchange transactions for common stock. Assets and liabilities are recorded at book value, the idea being to record the combined businesses as if they have been one ongoing business. Typically, but not always, earnings of the combined company will be higher under the pooling of interests method.

Several other questions are important to ask, and to answer, after the merger is announced. Does the merger put undue strain on the finances of the company? Can the company afford the additional leverage? Are earnings per share significantly diluted as a result of issuing more securities? Given conservative projections, what will earnings be over the next five years? Finally, if the merger looks healthy from the acquirer's point of view, are the terms offered to shareholders of the acquired company fair and acceptable?

How Valuable Is the Acquired Company?

Fundamental research is critical to any analysis of a merger deal. First, the price being offered should not be out of line with the real value. Second, a sound estimate of the company's potential value will help an arbitrageur assess the risk if the merger should fall through and determine how far the price could fall. Many companies to be acquired are researched closely by Wall Street analysts. The arbitrage departments of major firms, of course, have immediate access to their own research analysts. Independent arbitrageurs typically will have developed relationships with brokerage firms that have broad research departments. Standard and Poor's Corporation, and Moody's Investor Service are among those research firms that have considerable and publicly available information on thousands of companies.

But the arbitrageur also will make an independent and thorough fundamental analysis of the company. The arbitrageur will immediately acquire the latest public financial statements, annual reports, and Form 10-Ks (filed by all companies with the Securities and Exchange Commission). All available research reports will be gathered on the company and also on the industry. Again, while Wall Street research departments often are the best source of information about industry-wide and broad economic trends, arbitrageurs also will contact trade associations, independent economic consultants, and, as frequently as is possible, financial, legal, and economic experts in the home regions of the companies themselves.

Fundamental analysis will revolve around three general financial criteria.

1. Book Value per Share of the Company

Book value is defined as total assets less total liabilities (net worth). Book value per share is calculated by dividing by the number of common shares outstanding. But analysts must look beneath the reported numbers. In the 1970s, book value on the balance sheet often understated the value of a company's assets. Replacement values for industrial plants and factories were far higher during the inflationary 1970s and 1980s than their values as recorded on the books at original cost minus depreciation. Oil and natural resources also were typically understated. Arbitrageurs should do independent analyses of these assets. On the other hand, there are occasions when assets are not as valuable as they appear to be. The accounts receivable might be questionable, for example, or plants might be outmoded.

2. Earnings Projections

Earnings for large companies usually can be thought of as a function of industry growth and market share. The arbitrageur will explore both these areas. Companies often will have several products; an industry analysis and likely trend of growth will have to be made. Similarly, the position of that company in its market will have to be assessed, whether market share is shrinking or likely to expand. The earnings of natural-resource companies will depend greatly on the current prices for those commodities. An arbitrageur will have to make a judgment about the future course of these prices. Some companies, such as aerospace firms, are dependent on government orders that cannot be counted on in the future. A reasoned judgment again must be made about the future demand for such products. A five-year earnings projection in which the arbitrageur has confidence is an important part of the overall deal analysis.

3. Financial Health

An analysis of the company's liabilities also is a requisite step in the overall arbitrage decision. Conventional ratios should be examined, as well as the magnitude of debt charges and the schedule of loan and debt repayments. Pension liabilities and other off-balance-sheet liabilities should be assessed. Analysis of cash flow is critical. Is the company to be acquired a user or supplier of capital? The acquiring company, in fact, may have sufficient capital to support an expansion program that holds great promise. On the other hand, a merger might leave both companies relatively capital short.

Once these analyses are made, the arbitrageur can determine whether the terms of the merger are sensible. Generally, of course, the offering price will be substantially higher than the current stock-market price. Does the premium make sense in light of the company's real book value? In light of the firm's current and prospective price-earnings multiples? Could factors in the overall economy adversely affect either company? It cannot be emphasized strongly enough that if the value of the company as determined by the arbitrageur is well out of line with the terms of the merger, a good arbitrageur will not participate in such a deal.

How Badly Do the Managements Want to Complete the Deal?

In its preliminary stages, and even well into its later stages, a merger can be terminated if the two parties disagree. And in any proposed partnership, whether it be marriage or a merger, there are bound to be disagreements. More important, there often are unexpected obstacles to even the least contentious merger. The respective managements must have the commitment to resolve such problems. While seeking information about the companies by interviewing important managers, the arbitrageur should be able to get a sense of the depth of commitment of the respective managements.

Harder evidence can be gleaned from the way in which the companies work together to meet legal and financial requirements. There are often personal, financial, career, and other incentives that might make a merger desirable for both managements. The management of the acquired company, for example, might hold substantial shares or options that will be much more valuable if the merger is completed. The management of the acquiring company might be embarking on an aggressive acquisitions campaign to which they are clearly committed. Similarly, the executive leading the acquisition program might be a rising star. On the other hand, an acquisition might be part of a management battle at the acquiring company that, if lost, could mean the termination of a merger. Or the management of the acquiring company might be forced into the merger for lack of other alternatives to keep their company healthy.

How Well Is the Merger Being Handled?

Every merger must fulfill intricate legal, regulatory, and financial requirements that demand a broad range of expertise. Have the respective managements sought the advice of competent specialists in fashioning a merger? Do they have the in-house capability to understand, analyze, and meet with alacrity their many obligations? A sizable merger may require the services of specialized legal counsel in New York and Washington as well as locally, an investment banker who understands the markets and the growing array of financial techniques that can be tailored most appropriately

to the merger, a proxy solicitor to meet reporting requirements to the regulatory agencies and to shareholders, and
occasionally even a public-relations firm to make sure the
investment community understands the offer and related
issues. In some cases, management is able to handle some
of these functions itself or one adviser can serve several
roles. But if the firms have not hired the best advisers available, it is an important warning signal that the merger itself
may go awry.

Is the Merger Compatible with the Current Nature of Merger Activity?

Wall Street, like most other busy streets of the world, has
its fashions. The arbitrageur would be foolish to ignore them.
Managements are most comfortable in effecting mergers according to criteria that "the best and the brightest" on Wall
Street are currently preaching. In the 1960s, the favorite
word was *synergy*, meaning that two appropriate companies,
due to enlightened management or bigger size, produce a
stronger entity together than each standing alone. (In other
words, the whole is worth more than the sum of its parts.)

By contrast, in the 1970s, inflation compelled corporations to seek to buy companies with such natural resources
as oil and copper at what appeared to be deflated prices in
the stock market. In many cases, the mergers made sense;
others did not. The good arbitrageur, of course, will avoid
deals that are not sound in principle. But the good arbitrageur also will be sensitive to the trends and biases on Wall
Street. In the 1980s, the bias on Wall Street is toward buying
natural-resource companies. Thus, the arbitrageur can afford
to be more optimistic that such mergers will be consummated, and a reasonable adjustment to probability is in order.
Similarly, the arbitrageur should be sensitive to possible
shifts in the tide and to the deal that is carrying the fashionable strategy too far.

What Can Kill a Deal

1) Antitrust Issues

The most significant risk to many proposed mergers is a violation of the antitrust provisions of the law (see Chapter 7). In the case of mergers, the Hart-Scott-Rodino Antitrust Improvements Act requires a waiting period of thirty calendar days during which two federal authorities, the Justice Department's Antitrust Division and the Federal Trade Commission, review the proposal. Within that time, one of the two agencies will issue a ruling whether the merger may or may not violate the law. In the case of tender offers, the waiting period is fifteen days. But the arbitrageur cannot afford to wait for the ruling. Indeed, on the date of the public announcement of a proposed merger, well before a ruling is made, the arbitrageur must try to come to a judgment about potential antitrust problems. The arbitrageur also must consider whether and when the antitrust questions will be resolved should objections by the federal agencies be raised. Over time, professional arbitrageurs become familiar with the intricacies of antitrust law. But many professional arbitrageurs consult legal counsel in order to help them make an informed and balanced judgment about potential antitrust problems.

2) Determined Target Management

In recent years, some managements of target firms have been willing to go to great lengths to retain control of their companies. Such strategies are usually only effective if the raiding company is not significantly richer than the target. A target can sell off assets, buy back shares, and go heavily into debt to ward off a buyer. If a management is determined enough, such extreme defenses can occasionally work to stop a merger.

3) Management Disagreements

Two strong managements may disagree about an essential aspect of a merger after the announcement. The arbitrageur must be alert to all such potential conflicts. To repeat a previous point: the level of motivation among the influential members of management must be gauged. The nature of the personalities involved also must be analyzed. Some executives are consistent and predictable, others are not. Promises that cannot be fulfilled by the acquiring company may come to light only after negotiations intensify. Open issues of disagreement before the definitive agreement is signed should be examined closely.

4) Shareholder Objections

The arbitrageur must be confident that the shareholders will not defeat the proposed merger when the votes are finally tallied. An analysis of who owns the stock, whether large blocks are controlled by dissenting parties, and whether there are controversial issues that might rally shareholders against a merger must be performed.

5) Other Bids

A higher bid for the target company from another is often welcome to the arbitrageur who has a long position in the target company. But when the arbitrage position involves both a long purchase of the acquired company and a short sale of the acquiring company, a competitive bid is dangerous. The arbitrageur may be forced to cover the short position at a significant loss, especially if all arbitrageurs are covering their positions at the same time.

6) An Unexpected Change in Prices

The stock price of either the acquiring company or the target company or both can change dramatically for a number of reasons. Unexpected information about a company's business and an event in a company's industry might result in a significant fall or rise in the price. General market conditions also can change swiftly, sending most stock prices higher or lower. A sudden shift in interest rates or, more likely, a prolonged but substantial move in rates over a few months can sharply change the value of a package of securities that include debt instruments or preferred stock.

These changes can endanger a proposed merger. The acquiring company may not be willing to pay a higher price or may have changed its opinion about the value of the company. The company to be acquired may no longer find the offer as desirable. At the very least, a significant shift in prices can alter the terms of the merger, to either the advantage or disadvantage of the arbitrageur. This is the only area where market risk can play a role in classic merger arbitrage.

7) Ad Hoc Problems

Every proposed merger contains the seeds of unexpected and even unprecedented problems. The arbitrageur must keep a keen eye out for such events. Also the nature of the analysis once such an issue arises may have no precedent. The arbitrageur will have to assess the problem for the first time. Merger proposals have collapsed for such diverse and unanticipated reasons as disclosure of sensitive information about an officer of a company, failure to meet the technical requirements of federal agencies, or the offer or selling shares back to the company in a private transaction called "greenmail."

Sources of Information

Over the years, because of new regulations and legislation, information concerning merging companies is easier to obtain more quickly. Securities and Exchange Commission regulations concerning information in proxy and tender-disclosure material have made the arbitrageur's job far easier. In the past, merging companies submitted their proxy material to the Securities and Exchange Commission and had to wait up to several months before it was cleared and released to the public. Companies now are allowed to file a preliminary prospectus, Form S-14, that is immediately available to the public. The professional arbitrageur usually will have someone on hand at the Securities and Exchange Commission in Washington, D.C., to receive a copy of the S-14 within minutes of its release.

Proxy Statement

A proxy statement must be mailed to all shareholders in any announcement of any meeting or vote about a corporate reorganization. Information that accompanies the proxy material is closely regulated and must be cleared by the Securities and Exchange Commission. All relevant information to the proposed business transaction must be disclosed according to the Securities and Exchange Commission ruling. This generally includes historical and pro forma financial statements, complete summary of the terms, and disclosure of any other important information.

If included in an S-14, the preliminary proxy can be filed immediately with the Securities and Exchange Commission and is available to the public. Because of a loophole in the rules, if the preliminary proxy is not filed in an S-14, it will not be publicly available until cleared by the Securities and Exchange Commission. This document usually will contain all important information that will be in the final proxy as well.

Prospectus

According to the federal securities laws, public disclosure of information must accompany the issuance of any new securities. The prospectus represents this information and must be filed with and cleared by the Securities and Exchange Commission, much as proxy material is. A prospectus will be filed for a merger if the issuance of new securities is involved. Again, comprehensive financial statements, detailed descriptions of the companies, and the disclosure of all pertinent information is required by the Securities and Exchange Commission.

Annual Reports, 10-Ks, and 10-Qs

Most major companies publish annual reports and quarterly financial statements. The Securities and Exchange Commission requires that public companies file an annual report of their operations. That report is found on Form 10-K. Publicly held corporations also must file quarterly financial statements on Form 10-Qs. The public can obtain these forms from the Securities and Exchange Commission. Annual reports also are available from the companies themselves. Services are available that can provide annual reports, 10-Ks, and 10-Qs within a couple of hours of request.

S&Ps, Moody's, and Wall Street Sources

A great deal of information is available from Wall Street research firms. Standard and Poor's and Moody's publish updated analyses of a wide variety of corporations. Public libraries and most financial firms subscribe to these services. Wall Street research departments, which privately cover hundreds of corporations, can usually provide sophisticated research to their clients quickly.

Buying and Selling the Position

To the professional arbitrageur, the ability to buy and sell sizable positions efficiently is very important. Generally, arbitrage firms have their own trading operations. A skilled trader can save valuable fractions of a point per share. Managing short positions also is difficult. Stock must be borrowed and short sales can only be made on upticks, when the last sales price exceeds the previous price. As risk arbitrage has become more widespread, it has become harder to find stock to borrow. Speed of execution is important; professional arbitrageurs therefore use independent floor brokers to help execute a trade.

Options and financial futures have become important new tools for the arbitrageur. Options to buy stock (calls) or to sell stock (puts) allow the arbitrageur alternative means to take a position, often at lower capital charges. Using options can significantly reduce the capital needed, thereby enhancing potential return on capital; it also may provide the arbitrageur with a wider spread. Interest-rate futures, too, can be used to lock in, at least approximately, rates on debt or convertible issues that are part of a merger package. Today's sophisticated arbitrageur must be knowledgeable in the use of options and other new financial techniques (see Chapter 8).

The size of a position is a function of many factors, as we have seen. The arbitrageur must determine the potential return and the risks of the deal. These criteria must be compared to other arbitrage deals available for investment. Often an arbitrageur will seek to spread his risk over several deals, even though they are not equivalent in risk or potential return. There are margin and capital restrictions that may differ from deal to deal. There are also practical trading limitations on the size and speed with which positions can be taken or unwound, as well as on the availability of stock to cover short sales. In order to reduce risk, diversification is an essential part of an arbitrage operation.

The use of short sales provides not only a basic arbitrage hedge, but important tax advantages as well. Losses from short sales can be used to offset short-term capital gains. An arbitrageur also can hold his long position for the necessary term in order to qualify for long-term capital gains treatment. In addition, he may hold the short position and use the loss on the one transaction to offset gains on the other for tax purposes. But the arbitrageur must carefully abide by the intricate tax laws. Expert consultation is required here.

When the merger is at last effective, the arbitrageur must eventually extricate himself from two positions. He must cover his short sales and sell his long position. Typically, the arbitrageur will use the shares he received from the acquiring company for his position in the target to cover short sales in the acquiring company. The arbitrageur who implemented the basic merger arbitrage transaction in the first example in Chapter 2 sold short 1.25 shares of Company A for each share purchased of Company B. When the merger is completed, he will precisely cover the short position.

There are several technical aspects to selling positions. At times, so many shares come to market after a merger that trading opportunities develop. Savvy arbitrageurs often take advantage of this temporary imbalance of supply and demand. At the point at which a merger is declared bona fide by the New York Stock Exchange, an important capital advantage arises. The exchange disbands some of its capital requirements (this is known as the short exempt ruling). So the arbitrageur can buy Company B and sell Company A for much lower capital requirements.

Summary

To determine whether or not a merger will go through is essentially subjective. But there are fundamental questions that can be applied to all prospective mergers. A merger must make good business sense. The price being paid should not be unduly high compared with the worth of the company. There should be no serious antitrust barriers. Nor should there be obvious grounds for disagreement between the two managements. Finally, any ad hoc problems must be addressed. An investor therefore must know all pertinent public information about the two companies involved.

5
CASE STUDY

Now we are ready to apply all the fundamental tools we have learned to an actual case. I have chosen a merger that occurred in the mid-1970s to demonstrate the basic aspects of merger arbitrage. In many ways, General Electric Corporation's acquisition of Utah International for stock was a classic merger. It also came at a time when risk arbitrage was not widely practiced. A chronology of events on page 73 should be followed closely by the reader.

General Electric is, of course, the large and well-respected manufacturing company. Utah International was basically a copper mining company, but it also had substantial uranium holdings. The economic environment of the time must be understood. OPEC had quadrupled the price of oil in late 1973 and 1974. The world was stunned and confused by the price hike. It soon became clear that we had entered a new age of inflation. Corporate America was determined to protect itself from inflationary shocks. One way to do that was to own hard commodities.

Utah International was one of the more successful copper mining companies in the world. Copper's price is typically sensitive to rising inflation. General Electric's principal businesses had suffered badly in the deep recession of 1974 and the company was anxious to protect itself from the vicious cycles of inflation. Management settled on the acquisition of a copper company.

On December 16, 1975, General Electric announced its plan to acquire Utah. The terms were mutually agreed to by both parties. General Electric would pay shareholders of Utah International 1.3 shares of General Electric for each share they held. The first step for the arbitrageur to determine whether he should invest in this deal is to compute the workout value.

Workout value = 1.3 × General Electric stock price

On the day of the announcement, General Electric's shares closed on the New York Stock Exchange at $46^7/_8$. Plugging into our equation,

1.3 × General Electric stock price = 1.3 × $46.875 = $60.94

The workout value of the offer if cashed on that day would be nearly $61 a share.

The next step is to compute the spread. Utah's stock barely rose that day. It closed at $49^1/_8$. We will shortly discuss the reasons why it did not rise more. But first, let's note that the spread on the day of the announcement was nearly $12.

Spread = workout value − Utah price = $60.94 − $49.13 = $11.81

Now, we compute the rate of return on capital. Here are the five elements of the return on capital calculation, as outlined in Chapter 3:

1. Terms of the deal—workout value
2. Timing

3. Cost of money
4. Capital invested
5. Tax liability

We have already worked out the terms of the deal and determined the spread. Let's come back to the timing issue later, because that proved to be the most difficult to assess.

For ease of calculation, let us assume that our cost of money at the time was 12 percent. Similarly, for ease of calculation, we assume the arbitrageur can borrow for both long purchases and short sales up to 50 percent of the price of the shares. In reality, on the short side of a transaction, we could improve the leverage. Finally, the exchange of shares was tax-free to Utah shareholders. I had my accountants assure me that the exchange qualified under Internal Revenue Service rules.

On the day of the announcement, then, this is what the potential rate of return looked like for an investment of 100 shares. Remember, the arbitrageur's objective is to lock in that $12 spread by implementing the basic merger-arbitrage transaction. It would be the following:

Buy 100 shares of Utah International @ $49^1/_8$ = $4,912.50
Sell short 130 shares of General Electric @ $46^7/_8$ = $6,093.75

As we assumed, the arbitrageur only has to put up half the capital or $5,500. The interest cost at 12 percent a year would come to $660. And the profit is the spread of about $12 multiplied by 100 shares.

Now let's return to the issue of timing. A typical "friendly" merger might take four months between the announcement and completion of the deal, or the time you get your money. If we assume that this will be true for this merger, then we can make our final rate of return calculation.

Spread = $11.81 × 100 shares = $1,181
Capital = $5,500
Cost of money = $660 × $1/3$ (over four months) = $220
No tax liability
Return on capital = ($1,181 − $220) ÷ $5,500 = 17.5%

In other words, in four months the arbitrageur would earn 17.5 percent on his money if the merger went through as planned. On an annual return basis, we multiply by three.

Annualized rate of return = 17.5% × 3 = 52.5%

Thus, the arbitrageur who invested on December 17, the day after the merger was announced, could earn a very handsome 53 percent or so on his money if the deal went through smoothly in four months. But then why didn't investors push up the price of Utah? One reason is that there were then few savvy arbitrageurs and far fewer takeover-minded investors. The total value of the deal was nearly $2 billion, so the market could absorb a lot of buying before the stock price was forced up. This is the ideal condition for the arbitrageur.

But more important, on the day of the announcement, the Justice Department said that it was "looking into" the merger. Why? General Electric manufactured equipment for nuclear energy. And Utah was a prime supplier of the nuclear fuel, uranium. So there may have been grounds to bar the merger on antitrust considerations.

How does one analyze this risk? That became the primary concern of the arbitrageur. At best, the completion of the deal would be delayed significantly. And when the Justice Department did announce two weeks later that it would investigate the merger, Utah's stock price fell about 3 points.

According to most of our other criteria, this merger looked like it should go through. First, the economic environment was right. The fear of inflation was in the air. General Electric's business was badly hurt by the 1974 recession and the inflation that preceded it. Copper would be a good hedge. And at the price General Electric was paying for Utah, the deal made sense at the time—that is, if inflation continued on its course.

What I believed this deal had going for it most, however, was the determination of the General Electric and Utah managements. General Electric was not the sort of company that would back off easily. And it was interested in Utah for its copper, not its uranium. So I believed, in consultation with my antitrust law advisers, that General Electric could probably work out a deal to rid itself of Utah's uranium in order to allow the merger to go through.

But I did not buy the shares aggressively until a definitive agreement was announced. In mid-February, a definitive agreement was at last presented to the directors of both companies. They approved it one month later. The agreement was not signed until May 1976. The price of Utah had risen to $55^1/_8$ by then. Still, no one had heard from the Justice Department about the antitrust issue.

Let's take a look at what the spread was in May. At that point, General Electric was selling for $50^7/_8$. The workout value came to about $66^1/_8$. With Utah selling then at $55^1/_8$, the spread still was an attractive $11. In other words, if the arbitrageur implemented the basic merger arbitrage transaction by buying 1 share of Utah and selling short 1.3 shares of General Electric, he could still lock in a spread of $11 a share. Capital costs had risen to about $6,000. If the deal were completed four months from that point, the annualized return would still have come to about 43 percent. The point to be emphasized here is that *the arbitrageur must recompute the rate of return at each step along the way.* I invested heavily in May, buying Utah and selling General Electric short.

But there were more surprises to come. They form a good illustration of the ad hoc nature of risk arbitrage; one must be able to assess problems never faced before. There were price-fixing charges raised in the uranium industry. It was a complicated issue and the Justice Department said it would investigate this matter as well as the original antitrust issue between General Electric and Utah. But I concluded that the merger ultimately would not be affected by the price-fixing charges. The two companies publicly reiterated their desire to merge. The motivation of management is often the most important criterion. But at the least, there would be renewed delays. And to the arbitrageur, as I have stressed, time is money.

It took until October of that year, five months later, for the Justice Department to work out a plan that overcame the antitrust objections to the merger. Utah's uranium business would be transferred to a new company that was owned but not managed by General Electric. The merger would go through, the companies announced, by year's end. General Electric decided it could deal with the price-fixing issue, so that did not deter it from making the acquisition. On December 20, the merger of General Electric and Utah International was completed.

Because of delays, this merger deal was not as profitable for arbitrageurs as many others. But even if the arbitrageur had bought on the day of the announcement and waited a full year for the completion of the deal, he still would have earned about a 9.5-percent return. I've chosen this example to emphasize the ongoing nature of risk arbitrage and that the rate of return and the likelihood of the deal going through must be continually reassessed. Although the merger took a year to consummate, there were plenty of opportunities to invest late in 1976 and still make money. The day before the Justice Department resolution, for example, there was still a spread of some 10 points to be earned. And from that point, the deal would be completed in less than three months. This merger deal was so big, and the arbitrage community not yet fully developed, that the opportunities were constant. I unwound my position by using the new General Electric shares to cover my short position in the stock.

One last example of a straightforward arbitrage play may prove useful. It shows how quickly an arbitrageur must now act to exploit fully his opportunities. In November 1981, Beckman Instruments and Smith-Kline Corporation announced that they would merge for an exchange of stock. (A chronology of events is on p. 76 and should be followed closely by the reader.) Each Beckman share would be worth 0.7535 of a Smith-Kline share. With Smith-Kline selling at $64^1/_4$ after the announcement, the workout value was about $48.40. While Beckman was selling around 30 before the announcement it had since moved up to 43. The merger would be consummated in slightly more than three months. The final price of Beckman was $48^5/_8$ on the day the deal was completed. You should be able to calculate the rates of return for the arbitrageur on this transaction, had he acted fast enough.

Case Study:
General Electric and Utah International

Date	Action	NYSE Closing Prices Utah International	NYSE Closing Prices General Electric
12/15/75		$47^1/_4$	47
12/16/75	General Electric plans to acquire Utah International. 1 share Utah = 1.3 General Electric. Value of merger is $1.9 billion.	$49^1/_8$	$46^7/_8$

Date	Action	NYSE Closing Prices Utah International	General Electric
12/16/75 (Cont.)	Justice Department "looking at" proposed merger. General Electric says it has asked Justice for an opinion.		
12/29/75	Justice Department says it will investigate.	46³/₄	45³/₄
2/13/76	Definitive agreement to be presented to directors shortly.	51³/₄	51⁵/₈
3/16/76	Utah International directors approve merger.	51³/₄	51¹/₂
3/26/76	General Electric directors approve merger; agreement to be signed in April.	54³/₄	53¹/₂
5/19/76	Agreement signed.	55¹/₈	50⁷/₈
7/1/76	Both companies say merger still progressing.	57	57¹/₂
7/7/76	Justice Department is studying price-fixing in uranium industry.	59¹/₈	57¹/₂
7/23/76	Justice Department refuses to say it won't challenge merger.	59¹/₈	57¹/₂
7/27/76	Both firms say they will keep trying to proceed with merger. They "will work with" Justice Department.	58	54⁷/₈

Date	Action	NYSE Closing Prices	
		Utah International	General Electric
10/1/76	Friday.	$59^1/_8$	$53^3/_8$
10/2/76	Justice Department will not oppose merger. Utah's uranium business is to be transferred to a new company, owned by General Electric, but not controlled or managed by General Electric. Merger is to be closed by year end.	—	—
10/15/76	Westinghouse sues uranium producers over price fixings.	$60^7/_8$	$50^1/_2$
10/19/76	Trading halted in Westinghouse, General Electric, and Utah International. Justice proposes modifications in consent decrees by General Electric and Westinghouse on turbine generators. Trading later resumes.	67	$53^1/_2$
12/15/76	Stockholders of both companies approve merger.	$68^1/_2$	$52^7/_8$
12/20/76	General Electric and Utah International complete merger.	$68^5/_8$	$52^7/_8$ ($52^5/_8$ on when-issued stock)

Case Study: Smith-Kline and Beckman Instruments

		NYSE Closing Prices	
Date	Action	Beckman	Smith-Kline
11/23/81		$29^3/_4$	$67^1/_8$
11/24/81		$34^1/_2$	$67^3/_8$
11/25/81	Beckman Instruments and Smith-Kline Corporation announce that their respective boards have approved a preliminary merger agreement. Terms: Each Beckman common share would be convertible to 0.7535 of a Smith-Kline common share. Deal valued at $1 billion.	43	$64^1/_4$
11/27/81		$44^3/_4$	$65^1/_8$
1/25/82	Boards of Smith-Kline and Beckman Instruments approve the final merger agreement providing for Beckman to become a subsidiary of a new company called Smith-Kline Beckman Corporation.	$46^1/_8$	$64^1/_8$
3/4/82	Beckman Instruments shareholders approve Smith-Kline acquisition. Effective date of merger.	$48^5/_8$	$64^5/_8$

6
TENDER OFFERS

In the United States the tender offer is a relatively recent takeover technique. There are several reasons why it has proved to be the most fast-paced and exciting tool for arbitrage transactions.

First, the tender offer is the principal weapon in waging battle to acquire a company that will not agree to a merger. The unsolicited or hostile tender became a common practice in the 1970s and bidding wars among competing acquiring companies often drove premiums to 60 percent and more above the original market price of the target company.

Second, a tender offer is typically the fastest of merger transactions. This also can make it useful in negotiated merger transactions. An acquisition valued in billions of dollars can be completed very quickly. Indeed, such a transaction can be completed in just twenty business days. In the early 1970s, before the advent of rules regulating tenders, such transactions sometimes were completed within a week.

Finally, despite the adoption of disclosure requirements, there is usually less information available to the public about the companies involved in a tender than in a traditional merger. The arbitrageur must use all his skills to make a judgment about the likelihood of the success of the transaction, and he must do this very quickly. Most arbitrageurs find the tender offer their most severe test.

The history of the tender offer reveals why some tenders succeed and others fail. That history is a tangle of financial sparring and government regulation that at times has seen the target company a helpless victim, and at other times has seen the first corporate bidder in a takeover contest either lose or be required to raise its bid. The experience of more than two decades of active tender-offer activity suggests that the target company rarely stays independent. This, of course, makes arbitrage attractive. The tender offer has been an extraordinarily successful means of takeover in most cases. The arbitrageur must, as always, be wary. In those relatively few cases where the target company has retained its independence, the losses have been large.

The Tender-Offer Cycle

A tender is the cash offer by a corporation, individual, or other legal entity made directly to the shareholders of another company in exchange for the shareholders' stock (either for all or part of their holding). The traditional use of tender offers was to buy minority interest in one's own company. During the 1950s the tender offer became a widespread takeover technique in Great Britain, mostly in hostile situations. The Company Act of 1948 in Britain had allowed the easier removal of the corporate board of directors—previously a difficult process to accomplish legally. The act cleared the way for a spate of unfriendly takeovers that eventually involved the normally genteel British financial establishment.

Until about twenty years ago, proxy battles were more common in the United States than hostile tender offers. Typically, a dissident slate of directors put forth a platform to shareholders and waged a campaign to be elected, in the hope of replacing the existing board.

The arbitrageur should know the general economic and financial conditions that favor some takeover techniques over others. Throughout the 1960s, the tender offer, both friendly and unfriendly, became a more respectable means of corporate acquisition. In the late 1950s and early 1960s, stocks were undervalued compared with earnings and assets, much as they later were to be in the 1970s. As the economy recovered after World War II, cash became easier to obtain. A tender offer was faster to effect than a proxy contest. Besides, proxy contests seldom succeeded. Incumbent managements could, and do, use the corporate checkbook to defend their positions while insurgents have to spend their own cash to mount an attack. Cash tender offers also became popular because they were initially unregulated by federal and state agencies and did not fall under the purview of the securities acts.

As the tender offer grew in popularity, however, there were calls for regulation. In 1968, Congress passed the Williams Act, sponsored by Senator Harrison A. Williams, Democrat of New Jersey, which instituted the first direct federal regulation of tender offers. The act placed a seven-day minimum waiting period on any tender offer before it could expire. It also provided the Securities and Exchange Commission with the authority to develop disclosure requirements for tender offers. The Williams Act is an amendment to the Securities Exchange Act of 1934. The new sections added were 13(d) and 13(e) and 14(d), 14(e), and 14(f). The rules under the act have been revised several times and will be discussed in greater detail later in the chapter.

The Williams Act was intended to be an evenhanded piece of legislation, carefully weighing the rights of shareholders against the need to protect the target company. Most observers agree that the act was fair and did not seriously deter future tender offers. When economic conditions shifted drastically in the 1970s, the tender offer was to become more popular than ever.

Inflation began to dominate all other economic factors in the late 1960s and throughout the 1970s. The oil embargo of 1973 and subsequent price spiral were the principal shocks. A sharp and sustained decline in stock prices also took place. The overall market no longer adequately reflected the cost to replace plant, equipment, and other assets of many companies. It often did not reflect the liquidation value of companies with substantial natural resource reserves. And at some periods in stock-market history, stock prices did not even reflect the magnitude of financial assets held by many corporations. With such deflated stock values, conditions were ripe for a boom in takeovers. It was simply far more economical to buy an existing company than to build a new plant.

Such an environment was particularly conducive to the cash tender offer. Corporations did not want to use their own undervalued securities in a merger exchange. In inflationary times, cash is the cheapest form of capital. Borrowed cash, which will be paid off in future deflated dollars, is still cheaper. Large companies' shares were selling so cheaply that the acquiring company had substantial leeway to make a generous bid, despite the inability to examine closely the books and businesses of the target company.

Tender-offer strategies also underwent considerable evolution in response to target companies' defensive acumen and regulations adopted by both state and federal governments. The evolution reveals just how rapidly the arbitrageur must adapt to new circumstances. The vernacular attached to the different tender strategies suggests how aggressive the unfriendly merger environment became in the 1970s and early 1980s. A description of the major types of tender offers follows.

The Saturday Night Special

In the early 1970s, the "Saturday Night Special" quickly became a successful takeover technique. The Williams Act originally required a minimum of seven calendar days between the time a tender was publicly announced and its deadline. (It is now twenty business days.) Investment bankers quickly realized that announcing a tender to management over the weekend would reduce the effective working time for a response. In effect, the acquiring company made a sudden grab for its prey. This quick strike, occurring most often on a Saturday evening, soon was dubbed the Saturday Night Special. It was very effective for several years. One of the most colorful cases of the technique was the battle between Colt Industries and Garlock, the first example of the Saturday Night Special. (A case history on page 82 should be followed closely by the reader.)

One week in November 1975, Colt, the firearms company and now a conglomerate, announced that it would make a public tender for all of Garlock's shares. Garlock had closed the day before at $22. Colt offered $32. The total value of the deal was only $77 million. There were few defenses open to Garlock. The tender would expire in just eight days. I did not believe that there was a chance of successful antitrust action. Garlock's stock rose the next day to nearly $31.

Garlock sought to defend itself by seeking a friendly offer from a third party. Such a third party is called a "white knight." AMF came to the rescue by eventually offering $40 a share worth of its own common stock for each Garlock share. That same day, Colt increased its bid to $35 in cash. Because the deal was small, arbitrageurs controlled a large proportion of Garlock stock. They would go with the highest bidder, which gave AMF a legitimate opportunity to take the company, even though the offer was in stock.

Oddly enough, however, the relationship between Garlock and its white knight cooled quickly. AMF became what some call a "gray knight," meaning a not entirely friendly rescuer. Garlock's management decided to side with the Colt offer, and arbitrageurs had little time to wait for another bidder to come along. The tender expired shortly. The merger was effected by the end of January, and arbitrageurs received their money two months after the tender was underway. The Saturday Night Special allowed little time for a real bidding procedure to take place.

Case Study: Colt Industries and Garlock

		NYSE Closing Price	
Date	Action	Garlock	Colt
11/17/75		22	$26^1/_4$
11/18/75	Colt offers to purchase Garlock common for $32 per share. Offer valued at $76.8 million, and will expire 11/26/75. Garlock has 2.4 million shares outstanding.	No trading	26
11/19/75	Garlock opposes takeover attempt, brings lawsuit against Colt seeking to enjoin offer.	$30^3/_4$	$25^7/_8$
11/20/75	Garlock's counsel motions for preliminary injunction to halt takeover citing violations of federal antitrust and securities laws, requests $50 million in damages.	31	$25^7/_8$
11/24/75	AMF bids for Garlock. Terms: $40 per share divided by the average closing price of AMF common on the NYSE for the period prior to the merger.	No trading	$26^7/_8$

Date	Action	NYSE Closing Price Garlock	Colt
11/24/75 (Cont.)	AMF closes at $19.75 per share, down 25¢. Colt announces increase in offer price of $3 to $35 per share, expiring 12/3/75. Deal now valued at $84 million.	No trading	$26^7/_8$
11/25/75	AMF directors approve decision to negotiate with Garlock. Shareholder meeting scheduled for January 1976.	No trading	$27^1/_2$
11/26/75	Garlock announces acceptance of Colt offer for $35 per share.	$35^3/_8$	28
12/7/75	Colt has acquired more than 90% of Garlock shares (2,210,000 shares).	—	—
1/23/76	Directors of Colt and Garlock approve Colt's acquisition of Garlock as a wholly owned subsidiary.	No trading	$34^5/_8$

Third-Party Bidders—the White Knight

The entrance of a third party into a bidding contest for a target company can make the tender offer particularly rewarding to the arbitrageur. A bidding contest often ensues, the original bidder coming in still higher and perhaps the white knight topping that again. Confidence that a white knight may enter the situation gives the arbitrageur considerable comfort. Finding a white knight has become the principal defense of target companies fighting against takeover; and it is a very successful defense technique.

Several factors in a tender-offer situation will make it more likely that a white knight can be found.

1. If the target company is significantly undervalued, a strong case based on fundamental financial and business information can be made that a higher bid is justified.

2. The target company should be of fairly broad value and not of interest only to a certain kind of company.

3. The larger the size of the target, the harder it is to find a white knight. It is clearly easier to find a company, or several companies, willing to take over a $500-million company rather than one willing and able to take over a $5-billion company. But billion-dollar deals became more practicable in the 1980s.

4. The advisers to the target company must be aggressive, sophisticated, and knowledgeable. A select group of investment bankers and lawyers are particularly adept at and well situated for finding white knights.

In a securities-exchange offer, the arbitrageur will typically buy the target-company stock and short the appropriate amount of the securities package being offered by the suitor. The spread is thereby locked in. No such hedging strategies are available in cash tender offers, which in recent years have dominated all tender offers. Typically, exchange offers are friendly, but occasionally an unfriendly securities offer is undertaken.

In the depths of the 1973–1974 stock-market decline, corporations became particularly vulnerable to the quick tender offer. In response, many states, in order to protect their local corporations, and to attract defense-minded corporations to the area, adopted anti-takeover statutes that called for longer waiting periods and prenotification requirements. Two states had such statutes in 1969; less than ten years later, thirty-eight states had such laws. Fierce lobbying by local companies caused state legislatures to adopt these measures. By the mid-1970s, the effectiveness of the Saturday Night Special had diminished. The first corporate bidder often lost the contest to a white knight, another corporate bidder that was more friendly to the target company. The delays imposed by state laws provided enough time for an effective auction procedure to take place and for the target company to seek out white knights.

The Bear Hug

As the Saturday Night Special lost its effectiveness, a new technique, dubbed the "bear hug," achieved a limited success. The acquiring company would simply send a letter to the target company's board of directors that offered to buy the company at a significant premium above the current market. The directors were reminded that they had a "fiduciary responsibility" to the shareholders to accept the bid in their interest. Often the directors felt they were obliged to make the letter public. In other words, they were squeezed (or bear hugged) into submission. An example of the successful use of the bear hug follows. (A detailed chronology can be followed by the reader on page 86.)

Exxon Corporation's 1979 bid for Reliance Electric Company began with a letter to management making a bid for the company. The letter was received, the information made public, and the stock price rose. Reliance soon agreed to the merger.

What complicated the process was a surprise antitrust suit by the Federal Trade Commission. A solution eventually was found by segregating the business in question. But the result was that the merger was not effected for more than six months. That delay cost the arbitrageur money, although the spread was handsome throughout the deal. Note also that Exxon made a bid for Reliance's preferred stock. Profit was to be made on these shares as well.

Case Study: Exxon and Reliance Electric

| | | NYSE Closing Prices | | |
| | | Exxon | Reliance | |
Date	Action		Common	Preferred
5/22/79	Reliance Electric says it hasn't received an Exxon bid, raises questions on takeover.	52$\frac{1}{8}$	44$\frac{3}{8}$	124
5/24/79		50$\frac{5}{8}$	48$\frac{1}{4}$	128
5/25/79	Exxon formally announces a $72 per share tender offer for Reliance.	50$\frac{7}{8}$	60$\frac{5}{8}$	171
5/29/79	Exxon's offer for Reliance Electric of $1.17 billion is seen succeeding; Reliance's board might not oppose $72 a share. Terms of deal: Enco, a subsidiary of Exxon, will pay $72 a share for Reliance common and $202.72 a share for Reliance Series A Preferred Stock. Expiration date: 7/13/79. Shareholder meeting slated for 12/27/79.	50	62$\frac{1}{4}$	170
6/12/79	Exxon's takeover bid is called a bold stroke but is politically risky; its entry in motor industry is likely to spur drive for "excess profits" tax.	51$\frac{3}{4}$	61$\frac{5}{8}$	173

Date	Action	Exxon	Reliance Common	Preferred
			NYSE Closing Prices	
6/13/79	Reliance Electric doesn't oppose Exxon's proposal; action by board clears way to begin tender offer valued at $1.17 billion.	50	$60^{1/2}$	172
7/3/79	Exxon says FTC may halt takeover.	$53^{1/8}$	$58^{1/4}$	162
7/27/79	Friday.	55	$61^{1/4}$	166
7/28/79	U.S. District Court issues a temporary restraining order on application by the FTC. Agency also asks for preliminary injunction citing antitrust violations.	—	—	—
7/30/79	Exxon's purchase of an Ohio concern blocked by court. Reliance Electric takeover is restrained for ten days at the request of FTC.	$54^{7/8}$	$59^{1/8}$	163
8/17/79	Friday. Court requires segregation of motor and drive business; temporary restraining order expires; Exxon delays.	$53^{3/4}$	65	185
8/18/79	Court curbs takeover by Exxon; bars any action of Reliance to sell motor control.	—	—	—

Date	Action	NYSE Closing Prices		
		Exxon	Reliance Common	Preferred
8/21/79	FTC staff recommends that the government move to block Exxon acquisition of Reliance on the grounds that it would violate antitrust laws.	54³/₈	—	—
8/27/79	Hearing held to grant nonexclusive license by Exxon to third parties covering Reliance's ACS technology as an alternative to segregation provisions (ACS technology was the lure for Exxon's takeover bid).	56¹/₂	57	160
9/19/79	Reliance sues to force Exxon to purchase tendered shares.	57³/₈	61	175
9/24/79	Exxon proceeds with tender offer, announces termination of discussions with FTC regarding antitrust proceedings. Acquires 93% of Reliance common and 74% of Reliance preferred stock.	58⁵/₈	68⁷/₈	175

Date	Action	NYSE Closing Prices		
		Exxon	Reliance Common	Preferred
10/26/79	Court orders that Exxon segregate only the drive group of Reliance.	56¼	68⅜	194
10/29/79	Exxon elects six members to Reliance twelve-man board. Agreement of merger approved. Same terms. Total cost of merger for Exxon: $107 million.	56¾	68½	194
12/27/79	Effective date of merger.	55¼	71½	205

Open-Market Purchases

After a rise in bear hugs, however, it soon became clear that a board of directors' fiduciary responsibility did not extend to immediate acceptance of a high bid from a corporate suitor. Lawyers came to agree generally that the directors must only in "good faith" reach a business judgment regarding the desirability of the transaction, and the courts supported this view. A premium above market at a time when business conditions were cyclically poor and the stock market deflated did not necessarily mean that acceptance of the bid was in the shareholders' best interest. The bear hug was no longer effective.

As I have mentioned, tender offers are subject to federal and, to some extent, state regulation. Mere purchases of stock, either in privately negotiated transactions or in open-market purchases, are not subject to similar regulation. Aware of this loophole, prospective acquirers began to purchase stock in the targets before taking any further aggressive action. This tactic became known as the creeping tender. Such tenders were quite common in the hostile merger battles in England throughout the 1950s.

A corporation, for example, might buy 5 percent, sometimes more, of a potential target before it finally decided to go with a tender. (Section 13(d) of the Williams Act requires that a purchase of 5 percent or more be made public.) The advantages of this approach are twofold. First, the acquirer has a substantial portion of stock, which might give it an edge in a fight for control. Second, the cost of acquisition has been reduced at the start, because the acquired shares were bought at the prevailing market price. In addition, the bidder profits if a white knight enters the contest and forces up the bid. At the least, the first bidder will have earned a profit on the original stake if it loses the company. In other words, its stake will be bought out with the rest of the company. Occasionally, management will buy out a hostile shareholder group even if there is no other bidder. When done at a premium, this is known as "greenmail."

The Esmark-Inmont contest in 1977 is a particularly good example of the creeping tender. (A detailed chronology can be found on page 91.) While Esmark ultimately would lose its takeover bid for Inmont, it would make a substantial profit in the process.

In January 1977, Esmark quietly bought up 6 percent of the shares of Inmont Corporation in the open market. The Securities and Exchange Commission, Section 13(d), does not require that this be made public until 5 percent has been accumulated. This gives the acquirer time to keep his purchases secret. One month later, Esmark made a public bid for the company. Inmont rejected the bid a couple of days later and started searching for a white knight. Esmark started buying more stock on the open market in an attempt to squeeze Inmont. A few months later it raised its bid to $25 per share from the initial offer of $22.50. Inmont was in effect forced to accept a merger proposal from one of several white knights who approached it.

In the end, Inmont's management went with Carrier Corporation. But Esmark went home with a nice consolation prize: Carrier paid Esmark $28.25 for its 9.5-percent stake. Esmark's average cost to acquire that position was far below Carrier's buy-out.

Case Study: Inmont, Esmark, and Carrier Corporation

| Date | Action | NYSE Closing Price | | |
		Inmont	Esmark	Carrier
1/14/77	Esmark buys 6% of Inmont—450,200 shares at $15.375 as "investment."	16⅛	33½	18⅜
2/17/77	Esmark offers Inmont cash merger proposal for $22.50 a share. Inmont shareholders to get alternative of cash tender offer or stock-for-stock tax-free merger on same $22.50 basis. Inmont says it will consider proposal.	17¾	32¼	16¼
2/22/77	Inmont rejects Esmark takeover proposal. Inmont, in a letter to shareholders, says other companies have expressed an interest in acquiring it.	21¾	31½	16½

		NYSE Closing Price		
Date	Action	Inmont	Esmark	Carrier
3/11/77	Esmark increases Inmont stock holdings to 9.5%.	22	32	16¾
6/3/77	Esmark reopens its bid for Inmont by raising its offer to $25 a share. Esmark indicates that if Inmont board opposes offer, it will attempt a tender offer anyway. Inmont board to promptly consider offer. Esmark files Schedule 13d.	No trading	33½	18⅝
6/6/77	Inmont board rejects second Esmark offer. Esmark says it will continue plans for tender in spite of rejection.	No trading	33¾	18⅝
6/14/77	Esmark files proposed tender offer.	23¼	33¼	19⅛
8/9/77		26⅛	31¼	16¾
8/10/77	Inmont board weighs three merger proposals. Asks NYSE to halt trading.	No trading	31¾	16⅞
8/11/77	Inmont and Carrier in merger pact. Two companies sign agreement to merge. Value of deal: $28.25 per share for a total of $244 million.	28¼	31¾	16
8/16/77	Carrier pays Esmark $28.25 a share for 9.5% Inmont stake.	28⅛	31¼	16

Two-Step Tender

As stock prices rose in the early 1980s, another tender technique became popular. The acquiring corporation would tender cash for a controlling interest in the target company, usually 50 percent, but sometimes less. Once acquired, the suitor would then merge the two companies with an exchange of securities at a lower value. The acquirer was able to reduce the cash costs and also to pay less for the remaining half of the company, usually with securities. An important example of this approach was United States Steel Corporation's acquisition of Marathon Oil Company in 1981, an extraordinary battle of competing bids and hostile acquisition plays. (A detailed chronology of this difficult deal can be found on page 94.)

Here we see two partial-tender offers, one of which also included a security to buy the remainder of the company. Mobil Oil Corporation initiated the bidding with a bid for two thirds of Marathon's outstanding shares at $85 per share. Three weeks later, U.S. Steel offered to buy slightly more than half of the shares for cash at $125 a share, but then offered a new debt security for the remainder. Over the course of the bids, the value of the notes would be quite volatile. It is a good example of the difficulty of evaluating new securities, and also of how such values can change over time. Securities, of course, can be hedged by the arbitrageur. But to hedge new issues, the arbitrageur has to wait until a when-issued market develops. By the same token, such new markets often provide excellent opportunities to take positions because they are inefficient. Prices can swing wide of their fair mark.

Eventually, the bidding in this deal involved Allied Corporation as well as Mobil and U.S. Steel. The antitrust authorities played an important role as well. The winner was U.S. Steel with its two-step tender.

Case Study: Mobil Oil, U.S. Steel, and Marathon Oil

Date	Action	NYSE Closing Prices		
		Marathon	Mobil	U.S. Steel
10/30/81	Mobil Oil seeks to purchase 40 million common shares of Marathon Oil at $85 per share. Offer valued at $5.1 billion, expires 12/11/81. Conditions: minimum of 30 million shares being tendered. Second step of plan follows with a swap offer of Mobil's thirty-year debentures valued at approximately $85 per share. 40 million shares is equivalent to 67% of Marathon's outstanding shares.	$67\frac{1}{2}$	26	28
11/2/81	Marathon opposes Mobil offer, cites offer as inadequate and a violation of antitrust provisions.	90	$25\frac{3}{8}$	$28\frac{7}{8}$
11/3/81	Court order temporarily restrains Mobil. Antitrust issues to be investigated.	$85\frac{5}{8}$	$25\frac{1}{4}$	29
11/12/81	Marathon seeks merger partner.	$81\frac{1}{2}$	$24\frac{7}{8}$	$31\frac{1}{2}$
11/18/81		77	$25\frac{1}{8}$	$30\frac{3}{8}$
11/19/81	U.S. Steel announces offer to purchase 30	$104\frac{1}{4}$	$25\frac{1}{2}$	28

Date	Action	NYSE Closing Prices		
		Marathon	*Mobil*	*U.S. Steel*
11/19/81 (*Cont.*)	million common shares of Marathon for $125 per share. Offer expires 12/17/81. Further terms of deal: after tender, the remaining stockholders would receive $100 principal amount of a proposed new issue of twelve-year, 12½% senior notes of U.S. Steel for each untendered share. U.S. Steel retains option to purchase 10 million Marathon shares (17% of outstanding shares) at $90 per share plus a limited option to purchase Marathon's Yates oil field in Texas for $2.8 million. Meanwhile, Ohio legislature blocks Mobil's bid by amending antitrust law. Marathon pursues suit against Mobil on antitrust grounds.	104¼	25½	28
11/20/81	U.S. Steel and Marathon agree to merger terms. Congress criticizes U.S. Steel plan— Justice Department expected to examine	107¼	25⅝	27¾

Date	Action	NYSE Closing Prices		
		Marathon	Mobil	U.S. Steel
11/20/81 (Cont.)	antitrust aspects, misuse of government tax reductions and regulation relaxation to aid declining industries (i.e., steel). Marathon announces a potentially significant oil find in the North Sea.	107¼	25⅝	27¾
11/23/81	Previous private offer by Gulf of $7.2 billion for Marathon turned down by management.	104½	25⅞	27½
11/24/81	Mobil receives 38% of Marathon shares; needs 50%.	106¾	26½	30½
11/25/81	Mobil wins ten-day halt in court on U.S. Steel bid. Purchases $15 million of U.S. Steel stock, files papers with FTC disclosing purchases.	105½	25⅞	29⅝
11/27/81	Mobil offers new bid of $126 per share for Marathon. Deal valued at $6.5 billion, expires 12/11/81. Restraining order amended permitting U.S. Steel resumption of tender offer.	107⅛	26⅜	29⅞

Date	Action	NYSE Closing Prices		
		Marathon	Mobil	U.S. Steel
12/1/81	Mobil bid halted on antitrust issue. Federal district court in Cleveland grants preliminary injunction. Allied Corporation discloses $6.5-billion offer for Marathon. Terms: cash and securities at $120 per share for 61% of outstanding stock plus an exchange of two shares of Allied for each remaining Marathon share (Marathon rejected the offer on 11/17/81). Allied remains interested should U.S. Steel bid fail.	100	$27^{1/4}$	$29^{3/8}$
12/7/81	U.S. Steel acquires 51% of 60 million shares of Marathon stock. Mobil's request for a preliminary injunction to block U.S. Steel is denied. Deal disclosed between Mobil and Amerada Hess that Hess purchase Marathon's marketing, refining, and transportation properties to help resolve antitrust issue.	$101^{5/8}$	$26^{3/4}$	$29^{3/4}$

Date	Action	NYSE Closing Prices		
		Marathon	Mobil	U.S. Steel
12/9/81	FTC opposes Mobil. Ninety percent of Marathon stock tendered to U.S. Steel, which could not buy the stipulated 51 percent until the withdrawal deadline on 12/14/81.	92½	26⅜	29¾
12/10/81	Mobil bids for 25% of U.S. Steel.	87½	25⅞	32⅜
12/14/81	U.S. Steel takeover barred by Cincinnati appeals court. Mobil extends expiration date to 12/31/81.	88½	25¼	31½
12/24/81	Judge allows U.S. Steel to resume purchase of Marathon after 1/6/82.	83¾	24⅝	31⅛
1/5/82	Mobil loses appeal to block U.S. Steel bid.	79½	24	29⅜
1/6/82	U.S. Steel expected to buy controlling interest in Marathon.	78	24⅛	29⅛
1/14/82	Class-action suit filed by two Marathon shareholders to block U.S. Steel merger, claiming unfair and inadequate price for twelve-year, 12½% senior notes for remaining untendered Marathon shares.	74¾	22½	26⅜

Date	Action	NYSE Closing Prices		
		Marathon	Mobil	U.S. Steel
1/14/82 (*Cont.*)	Shareholder meeting slated for 3/11/82. Negative vote of 20 million of Marathon's 59.1 million shares needed to block the merger.	74³/₄	22¹/₂	26³/₈
2/3/82	Mobil drops bid for U.S. Steel shares. Marathon proxy statement discloses notes worth $81–84 per 100 principal amount versus $86 valuation assumed by Marathon directors in November.	74	22³/₄	24
2/8/82	Another Marathon shareholder sues Marathon and U.S. Steel, alleging conspiracy to aid U.S. Steel offer.	73	21³/₄	22⁵/₈
2/17/82	Shareholder opposition builds regarding second half of U.S. Steel offer to swap 12¹/₂% notes. Appraisal proceedings threatened.	73³/₈	22¹/₈	23¹/₂
2/18/82	The Dreyfus Corporation (holder of 650,000 Marathon shares) announces intention to vote against U.S. Steel due to low valuation of notes.	73	22¹/₄	23¹/₂

Date	Action	NYSE Closing Prices		
		Marathon	Mobil	U.S. Steel
2/23/82	U.S. Steel holds firm on original offer. Supreme Court denies Mobil's final appeal.	73⅝	22⅛	23⅞
2/24/82	Plaintiffs in seven suits seek preliminary injunction to block Marathon shareholder meeting on 3/11/82.	73⅜	22⅜	24⅛
3/9/82	Dreyfus, Morgan Guaranty, and other institutional holders oppose merger.	75⅜	21⅞	23⅝
3/10/82	Judge rejects bid to block shareholder vote.	75¾	22⅝	23⅝
3/11/82	U.S. Steel acquisition passes at stockholder meeting (78% of Marathon shareholders vote yes). Marathon becomes a wholly owned subsidiary of U.S. Steel. Deal represents the second largest merger in history.	75⅝	25⅛	23⅜

The Partial Tender

It is common that an acquirer will bid only for a portion of the outstanding shares of a company. In the Mobil-Marathon merger, for example, U.S. Steel initially bid only for 51 percent of the shares. Companies also will announce bids for a minority of shares as well. Often a company will announce a tender offer for a stated portion of shares, and leave open the possibility that it will accept more shares if tendered to it. The company will not stipulate how many more.

The arbitrageur must calculate the value of shares he will tender. This is complicated because it is a partial tender. Not all his shares will be tendered. Instead, a prorated percentage will be accepted, the same proration for all tenderers. The arbitrageur computes what is called the blended value of the shares. The blended value is the sum of the value of the tendered shares and market value of the non-tendered shares.

An acquiring company may state that it is seeking 50 percent of all shares outstanding at $30 a share. Before the announcement, shares were trading at $20. If the arbitrageur assumes that all shareholders will decide to tender, then just half his shares will be accepted at $30. The other half are probably worth only $20, the price before the bid. The blended value is as follows:

$$\$30 \times \tfrac{1}{2} = \$15$$
$$\$20 \times \tfrac{1}{2} = \underline{\$10}$$
$$\text{Blended value} = \$25$$

The $25-per-share price is in effect the workout value. If shares are trading below that price in the open market, the arbitrageur might buy them.

But occasionally, companies will take more than the stated number of shares being tendered for. And seldom are all shares tendered. The arbitrageur must make assumptions about these factors to arrive at a blended value. Insider blocks, family ownership, and other loyal factions may not tender, and these shares should be totaled. The remainder of shares are in the hands of the public. Depending on the deal, it is usually fair to assume that most, but not all, shares will be tendered.

In the following example, the arbitrageur believes 75 percent of the outstanding shares will be tendered, and that the company will accept at most the stipulated 50 percent. Only two thirds of the arbitrageur's position will be accepted (50 percent is two thirds of 75 percent). The arbitrageur must then make an assumption about the price at which the remaining one third can be sold. In sum, he can expect to sell two thirds of this holding for the tender price and one third at the subsequent market price. To calculate the blended value of this partial tender:

Bid for 50% @ $30
Price before bid = $20
Current price = $25

After analyzing the shareholders, the arbitrageur believes that 75 percent of the shares will be tendered. Two thirds of the position will be sold for $30 and the remaining third for $20. The blended value then is:

$$\$30 \times \frac{2}{3} = \$20.00$$
$$\$20 \times \frac{1}{3} = \$\ 6.67$$
$$\text{Blended value} = \overline{\$26.67}$$

Several examples of the partial bid have already been described. The U.S. Steel two-step offer for Marathon is a good example. So is Texaco's acquisition of Getty Oil, which was discussed in the Introduction. Before Texaco entered the contest, Pennzoil bid $100 a share for 20 percent of the company. The price at the time was about $80. I assumed that Gordon Getty, who controlled 40 percent of all outstanding shares as head of the Sarah C. Getty Trust, would not tender, nor would the Getty Museum, which had more than 12 percent. Finally, I assumed that all but a handful of the remaining shares would be tendered. So, in total, about

50 percent or a little less of the outstanding shares would be tendered and Pennzoil would accept 20 percent (40 percent of those tendered) at $100 a share. The remainder would probably fall back to $80 a share.

The computation to determine the blended value is:

$$40\% \text{ of shares accepted at } \$100 = \$40$$
$$60\% \text{ of shares trade back to } \$80 = \underline{\$48}$$
$$\text{Blended value of partial tender offer} = \$88 \text{ a share}$$

Cash Tender Offers: The Legal Procedure

Cash tender offers are now subject to both federal and state laws, as well as to regulations established by various agencies. The importance of state regulations has been dramatically reduced by federal courts in recent years. The federal jurisdiction involves both the timing and procedure of tender offers, as well as the nature of the disclosure required. As with all mergers and acquisitions, the Hart-Scott-Rodino antitrust waiting period applies. For cash tenders, however, the waiting period is only fifteen calendar days (thirty calendar days are stipulated for other transactions). The ability to purchase shares in a cash tender can be delayed another ten days after submission of proper documentation to the antitrust authorities if additional information is requested.

The first federal legislation directed solely at tender offers, as noted, was the Williams Act, which was passed by Congress in 1968. The Securities and Exchange Commission also has rules regarding filing of information, dissemination of that information to shareholders, disclosure requirements, waiting periods, and prorating procedures. These rules have been revised several times over the years, but are still a complex web that must be carefully untangled.

Section 13(d) of the Williams Act requires that all individuals or "groups" owning 5 percent or more of a public corporation must report that information on a Schedule 13(d), which must be filed with the Securities and Exchange Commission and delivered to the target company.

Sections 14(d), 14(e), and 14(f) relate directly to the cash tender offer. Section 14(d) requires a filing by the acquiring company, prior to making the tender offer. The schedule requires a variety of information, including the name and employment of the buyer, source and amount of funds to be used in the acquisition, any arrangements with other persons regarding shares of the target company, information about past dealings between the bidder and target company, and future plans for the target. There also is a general request for any other information that might be relevant to the acquisition.

The rules provide several different methods of disseminating information to shareholders.

• The bidder requests the target's shareholder list. The target company chooses either to disseminate the offering materials itself or to give the bidder its shareholder list. Many states have laws that require companies incorporated in those states to furnish shareholder lists to a shareholder who requests them and who meets certain specified criteria. Typically, a bidder will request the shareholder list under both the applicable federal and state laws; since state laws generally don't give companies the alternative of mailing directly to shareholders, the bidder can usually obtain a reasonably current shareholder list.

• The bidder then has the choice either to publish the tender information in long form, which must include all required information, or to disseminate the materials by mailing to the shareholders.

• To begin the offer, the bidder can publish a short-form advertisement, so long as it is immediately followed up by the detailed tender-offer document.

Should the bidder choose to disseminate information using the stockholder lists, which is usually the case if the target releases the shareholder list, the following procedure is standard:

• The bidder requests the stockholder list from the target company.
• On that date, or prior to it, the bidder either publishes a short-form advertisement or a long-form publication, which serves to begin the offer.
• The target company decides whether to disseminate the materials itself or to supply the bidder with the shareholder list.

If the target company decides to disseminate the information itself, other rules pertain. Similarly, the bidder must follow prescribed rules if it uses the shareholder list.

The final important provision under the disclosure sections concerns the target company. If the target chooses to fight the bid, it also must file a disclosure document. The completeness and accuracy of the disclosure documents provided by both the bidder and the target are often the subject of litigation. But courts are loath to stop offers and generally permit any deficiencies in the documents to be corrected.

There are several sections in the Williams Act that provide waiting periods that significantly affect the duration of the offer. Section 14(e)(1) requires that a tender offer must remain open for a minimum of twenty business days. If the bidder raises the bid, or a competing bid is made, the tender must stay open for an additional ten days. Under Section 14(d), a shareholder who has tendered securities may withdraw them at any time during the first fifteen business days of the offer (the shares can also be withdrawn at any time after sixty days of the commencement of the offer).

The Williams Act also deals with the prorating process for partial tenders. If an acquiring company is bidding for, say, only 50 percent of the outstanding shares, at one point it had the option of accepting bids on a first-come, first-served basis, or on a pro rata basis. The first-come alternative was properly viewed as putting undue pressure on shareholders to tender to the first bidder. The rules now require that during the entire period of a partial offer, all shares must be accepted only on a pro rata basis.

The Arbitrageur's Considerations

The rate of success of the tender offer has been very high. Few target companies ultimately have remained independent. Annual surveys by *Merger and Acquisitions* magazine demonstrate that tender failures typically have amounted to fewer than 20 percent of bids made. Goldman, Sachs and Company periodically has undertaken its own surveys of larger tender offers. In these surveys, a distinct minority of the original targets ultimately remains independent. By contrast, unfriendly exchange offers have not been very successful.

Similarly, premiums bid over the current market price were generally handsome. W. T. Grimm and Company finds that they averaged nearly 50 percent since the mid-1970s.

But the arbitrageur must consider other factors in determining the success of his investment strategy. The loss that can result from a failed tender offer can be onerous. The time over which the tender offer can run is important as well in determining potential returns. It can be extended for a variety of legal and financial reasons. The analysis of the tender offer follows much the same procedure as it does for merger arbitrage. But there are important differences that have to do with timing, available information, taxes, and defensive maneuvers by the target company.

Fundamental Analysis of Target

It is critical that the abritrageur determine the value of the target firm as quickly as possible. Because little information on the target will be available in the tender disclosure material, the arbitrageur's first recourse are the annual report and the 10-K and 10-Q schedules filed with the Securities and Exchange Commission. Other public sources, as previously noted, include Standard and Poor's, Moody's, and other available Wall Street research.

The standard analysis will follow the steps outlined in Chapter 4. But in the case of tender offers, it is reasonable to assume that the bidder will have discovered, and covets, assets or other company attributes that are particularly undervalued, in its estimation, by the stock market. Often, the target company is well known and its valuable assets are no secret among Wall Street investors. And just as often, the target company is in an industry that already has proved fertile ground for takeovers. For example, in the 1970s, oil companies were attractive values—the professional arbitrageur generally had developed an expertise in quickly assessing the value of oil reserves. Similarly, several categories of natural-resource companies were popular takeover targets that arbitrageurs quickly learned how to evaluate. It must be emphasized that, like the arbitrageur, the unfriendly bidder generally has no more information about the target company than what is publicly available.

The characteristics of the target company have been mentioned briefly. According to a research report issued by the Conference Board in 1977, the most obvious characteristics that make a company vulnerable to a hostile takeover bid are:

1. Low ratio of stock-market price to reported book value.
2. Low price-earnings ratio.

3. Significantly undervalued assets in the ground, such as oil and natural resources.

4. Plant and equipment in a strong industry that has a significantly higher replacement cost than is reflected in the stock price.

5. Underlying real estate that is undervalued on the balance sheet (examples include retail chains that own their real estate, restaurant chains, warehouse companies, racetracks).

6. Valuable financial assets not reflected in stock price (there are occasions when cash plus current assets less all liabilities are greater than or equal to the stock-market value of the company).

7. High cash flow, or unused borrowing capacity.

8. Signs that the business will soon turn around from depressed levels of earnings.

9. Weak, entrenched management that could make better use of assets or possibly liquidate the company at a premium of market value.

Shareholder Analysis

Who the shareholders of the target company are is important in determining the success or failure of a tender offer and, to some extent, even the price. Large blocks of stock held by families or groups that for some reason may be particularly loyal to the company can and have caused the defeat of the tender offer. Some companies' shareholders are in large part made up of workers and local townspeople. Occasionally, large blocks of stock are in the hands of related holding companies or trusts. On the other hand, large ownership by financial institutions and foundations is conducive to a takeover. These institutions are generally obligated to take the greatest profit available, rather than decline on other grounds. Sometimes it is apparent that even management has a motive to sell. The exercise price of stock options, for example, may be less than an acquiring company's bid. Thus, management itself might have a large incentive to tender its own shares.

Insider holdings must be reported to the Securities and Exchange Commission.

The arbitrageur is interested in not only who owns the shares and in what quantity, but also the price at which they were acquired. A tender offer is much more likely to succeed if it provides a sizable profit to most investors. On the other hand, from an earlier buyer's viewpoint, a stock that has dropped from extravagant highs might find eager sellers merely if the stock returns to a break-even price. The average cost of insider holdings is disclosed in the form 10-K. The price at which many shareholders bought in the past can be deduced from trading volume.

Antitrust Questions

The arbitrageur must make a quick judgment about whether the tender offer will result in a business combination that the antitrust agencies—either the Justice Department or the Federal Trade Commisson—might challenge. Such a challenge could result in either a delay of the transaction (which might be costly to the arbitrageur) or the forbidding of the tender offer altogether. The Hart-Scott-Rodino Act calls for a fifteen-day waiting period to give the federal agencies time to determine whether the merger will be challenged.

The arbitrageur's capacity to make an accurate judgment of federal antitrust reaction to a tender offer is very important. Most professional arbitrageurs have one or more attorneys on call for advice.

The Justice Department does offer merger guidelines. Further, there frequently are related rulings to be examined. Moreover, the acquiring company will usually have done its own research into the subject and put forth its opinion in the disclosure material. Finally, even if there are antitrust objections, companies often can overcome them by selling the contested part of the business.

Still, the course of antitrust action is quite often terribly difficult to predict accurately. *And because a decision that a merger does violate the antitrust laws will abrogate the merger entirely, it represents the largest risk to the arbitrageur.* The problem is that the attitude toward mergers shifts over time and with different administrations in Washington. No arbitrageur can perform effectively without a comprehensive grasp of the law, the procedure of the federal agencies, and the predisposition of current powers in the nation's capital.

State Laws

The arbitrageur must immediately determine whether the tender offer falls under the jurisdiction of one or more states and whether the merger might violate those laws. A state usually has jurisdiction when the target company is based in that state. A state also may have jurisdiction if a large part of the company's business or manufacturing is done within it. The state court will decide whether it should take jurisdiction.

Most state takeover laws have been superseded as a result of the Supreme Court decision in *Edgar* v. *Mite Corporation* in 1982. Now most defense actions taken by targets under state takeover laws are no longer effective. But there are still occasions where a state can delay a tender offer. Again, the professional arbitrageur typically will have access to legal specialists on state laws, as well as local counsel within the state.

Summary

Time is the critical element in tender offers. An acquisition can be completed within weeks. For the arbitrageur, this means that the rate of return on such deals can be very high. It also means that decisions must be made quickly. The same analysis applying to a conventional merger that involves an exchange of shares also applies to tender offers. But there are other limitations besides time. Not as much information is required to be disclosed for most tender offers.

The nature of tenders has changed over the years. Today, the practice and schedule of tender offers is closely determined by federal law. These regulations must be well understood by the arbitrageur. But generally speaking, target companies seldom stay independent once a tender is made. An arbitrageur must assess the likelihood that a third party will enter the bidding and push prices higher. Tender offers are the principal vehicle used to launch hostile takeover contests.

7
DEFENSE

To every action there is a reaction. The art of defending corporate merger targets has become as complex, aggressive, and ingenious over the past decade as has the hostile cash-tender offer itself. The basic objective of the defense is to thwart the bidder and retain the target company's independence. Failing that, defense then embarks on a search for a friendly white knight to acquire the target company.

In practice, few corporate defenses actually succeed. But the successful arbitrageur must understand fully the defense procedures available to any company. The few defenses that have impeded a deal can be costly. This chapter will summarize such defense strategies.

The defense arsenal includes a broad array of legal and financial weapons, some traditional and others new, intricate, and constantly evolving. The awareness among corporate managers of the need to be able to defend against potential raiders is now widespread. The first step to protect a target company from a takeover bid is no longer taken only when the tender offer is made. Many corporate managements now take actions to defend against bids without an active threat on the horizon. Such actions include lining up experienced investment bankers and counsel; adopting so-called shark repellents, such as a staggered board of directors; and modifying employee-benefit plans to reflect potential control changes.

Anticipatory Defenses

The mere preparation of a plan of action should a tender offer be made has aided many companies in responding to a hostile offer. Essentially, such a plan outlines a basic course of action and assigns individual executives roles and responsibilities should it become necessary to carry it out. Some companies actually organize a defense team of top management and other personnel. Companies also prepare guides or manuals, known as black books, in case of tender offers. Perhaps the most important planning a management can do is to hire expert advisers. These will include attorneys that specialize in takeovers, investment bankers, proxy solicitors, and often public-relations firms as well as local legal counsel. Waiting to contact advisers until a bid is made can often cost valuable time. There are not many legal and financial firms that specialize in the field, and often they have conflicts of interest that will disqualify them from taking on a company as a client.

The so-called black book is quite straightforward. It often includes a list of managers and directors and their telephone numbers, step-by-step procedures for immediate response to a tender offer and disclosure requirements, and schedules that must be filed with appropriate federal or state agencies. Sometimes a variety of letters to be sent to shareholders may be prepared, although it is difficult to anticipate the varying circumstances a bid can present; therefore, canned responses can be embarrassing, at least from the point of view of future litigation. Management may quietly prepare a list of potential white knights. The names and telephone numbers of outside expert advisers are also included in a typical black book. Of course, the circumstances of each tender offer will differ and preparation of a plan of action beforehand is necessarily limited.

Devising a good plan is the first step in corporate defense, but management can take several explicit actions to make an acquisition more difficult. Many corporations implement a series of measures to make control changes more difficult and to protect minority shareholders. These actions generally require changes in the corporate bylaws and charter, which require shareholder approval.

Charter Provisions Concerning the Board of Directors

A number of measures can be taken to make it difficult for a substantial, even a controlling, stockholder to remove the board of directors. A common charter provision calls for the staggering, or classification, of the board of directors. Typically, the board is divided into three classes, each group serving three years. The New York Stock Exchange allows for a maximum of three classes. The controlling faction can then replace only one third of the board members at each election.

There are several measures that can be taken by a company to protect a classified board. Depending on state statutes, a company may adopt a bylaw or charter provision that requires that cause be shown before a director can be removed. Similarly, depending on state law, a supermajority (more than a simple majority) vote could be made a condition for the removal of directors. To circumvent the classified board, corporate raiders often will expand the size of the board and pack the resulting vacancies with sympathetic directors. To counter this tactic, a charter provision can be adopted that gives only the board the right to determine the number of company directors. This provision, in turn, can be made ironclad except by supermajority vote. Such provisions have been dubbed "shark repellents" by the financial community for obvious reasons.

In general, the New York Stock Exchange reviews these provisions. The Securities and Exchange Commission requires that disadvantages to the shareholders be adequately described in the proxy statement before the shareholder vote. Thus, the proxy material must state that these provisions can deter tender offers and serve to protect management.

Fair Price Provision

Provisions can be adopted by corporations that make it difficult or expensive to acquire the minority shares. The basic measure is known as the fair price provision. It requires that an acquiring company that owns, say, 10 percent of the target pay shareholders that have not tendered, or have been shut out, a specific minimum price—typically not less than the tender-offer price. This is designed to reduce the pressure on shareholders to tender early for fear they will be bought out later only at a lower price. It also raises the cost of a complete takeover. The two-step front-end-loaded takeover that became popular in the early 1980s is made less effective by such a provision. If the second-step bid does not meet the price standards, a supermajority vote is required for approval.

Shareholder Approval

Many corporations have adopted provisions that require that any merger with a substantial shareholder—anyone who owns 10 percent or more of the outstanding shares—must be approved by a supermajority vote. While a minimum of 75 percent of shareholders is typical, a supermajority provision can require as much as 90 percent. The vote is often designed to cover not merely a merger but a transfer of assets, liquidation, reverse splits, or any similar transaction that would increase the relative interest of a substantial shareholder.

However, these provisions can create unanticipated problems in turn. For example, they might impede a friendly merger approved by the board but opposed by a substantial shareholder. They also might impede an internal reorganization between the company and, say, a subsidiary. Such provisions, therefore, are usually accompanied by so-called escape clauses that make exceptions for these two cases. A few state regulations try to restrict sales of securities of companies whose charter or bylaws contain escape clauses.

Other Provisions

There are a variety of other measures designed to protect potential targets. One is the forbidding of surprise nominations of directors. Provisions have been adopted that require consideration of the social effect of a merger or that define the eligibility of certain entities to be shareholders. Loan agreements and other contracts sometimes are designed so that the agreement or contract can be broken if there is a change in management.

Special Management Compensation

A particularly popular practice has been to provide a company's top managers with long-term employment contracts or large severance compensation in case of a takeover. Wall Street has dubbed such measures "golden parachutes." They protect incumbent management and also serve to make the takeover bid more expensive to the acquiring company. Other employee benefit plans can be modified to reflect the consequences of a takeover, such as permitting otherwise non-exercisable options to be exercised more rapidly.

Other Anticipatory Defenses

Pre-bid defense tactics are not restricted to protective bylaw and charter provisions. Corporate managements particularly aware of their vulnerability as takeover targets have taken other direct and sometimes aggressive measures to safeguard their companies. These measures include financial and procedural tactics that have, for the most part, gained legal sanction.

Other Tactics

Corporations can develop procedures to monitor trading in their stock. Unusual purchases may presage a tender offer. Some companies have actively tried to anticipate likely corporate acquirers and to gather information about them that might be useful to fight a possible bid. Some companies also have tried to line up potential friendly third parties in case of a hostile takeover attempt. This course of action is risky: if pursued too vigorously, it arouses the interest of corporations that might choose to mount a hostile-tender offer themselves, instead of making an offer only if invited.

Financial Anticipatory Defense

Corporations often will try to correct or reverse those financial characteristics that make them particularly attractive takeover candidates. A company whose stock price is low may direct its efforts toward improving its price-earnings multiple through an investor relations plan, paying more attention to quarterly earnings growth and increasing its dividends. Such an objective is difficult to accomplish, of course, and must be weighed against the longer-term health of the company. Sometimes unduly conservative accounting methods might result, at least in the acquirer's mind, in a low stock price. The accounting practice can be changed.

In other cases a company that is attractive because of its high level of cash (a common situation in the 1970s) or its debt-free balance sheet will consider using its assets more energetically. Corporations have made acquisitions for cash, for example, largely as defensive moves against potential takeovers. A capital-spending program requiring long-term borrowing is another pre-bid defense if a company's attractiveness is essentially its healthy balance sheet. A change in capital structure also can accomplish the same ends.

Acquisitions also can be undertaken that raise difficult legal or antitrust obstacles in the event a takeover is attempted. A company that owns a federally regulated business, for example, is less vulnerable to takeover because government approvals must be obtained. At the least, this will entail delays that could be costly or cumbersome in a tender offer. A potentially vulnerable company will at times undertake such an acquisition. If the target corporation can anticipate the type of company that may seek to acquire it, management might consider acquiring a company in a related business to raise the specter of an antitrust obstacle to an acquisition.

The Initial Response

Once a tender offer is made public, corporate defense goes into full gear. Speed and money are generally the deciding factors. During the early 1970s, the duty and responsibility of the target company and its board of directors were not clear. Directors were concerned that their response to a tender offer might either breach their fiduciary responsibilities or be subject to the anti-fraud statutes of federal securities laws. Such lack of clarity, as was noted in Chapter 6, is what made the bear hug an effective takeover technique, if only temporarily.

In recent years, a body of case law has developed that has clarified the directors' rights and obligations. Moreover, the Williams Act has established explicit rules about the timing and disclosure of materials. It is generally agreed that the directors have the right to resist a takeover attempt as long as they act in good faith in the best interest of the shareholders.

Still, boards of directors must be careful that they exercise their business judgment in good faith. Responses must be carefully considered. The target company must take the following steps, according to federal law and the rules established by the Securities and Exchange Commission.

1. After having been requested to do so by the bidder, the target company must either deliver a shareholder list to the bidder or mail the tender offer materials directly to all shareholders.

2. Within ten business days, the target company must publish its decision whether it intends to accept or reject the bid, or whether it will not take a position, and its reasons.

3. When it takes its position, the target company must file a Schedule 14(d)(9) with the Securities and Exchange Commission. This form sets forth the directors' reasons for their recommendation, details any trading in the target securities, and describes any conflict of interest respecting the bid.

Typically, the target company will explain the board's position. The company also will often run advertisements in the *Wall Street Journal* and *The New York Times* with the same information. The argument for rejection usually claims that the bid is too low and outlines the financial prospects of the company. The advertisement notes that management will not tender its own shares, characterizes the tax consequences of the bid (the transaction is usually taxable), points out antitrust or other legal problems, and states any other critical information. Management also may initiate a public-relations campaign with the financial, national, and local press to try to disseminate its views.

Although case law, as noted, generally supports the board of directors' right to vigorously oppose a tender offer, discretion, care, and good faith are required. The following is a list of measures the board of directors may take in resisting a tender offer ("Defending Against Corporate Takeovers," a private paper written by Martin Lipton and Henry Lesser of Wachtell, Lipton, Rosen and Katz, New York, 1982).

1. Management should make a full presentation to the board of directors of all the factors relevant to the takeover bid, including historical and projected financial data; future capital spending and product plans; replacement value of assets; information about the timing of the sale; stock price data; antitrust, regulatory, or other legal issues; and an analysis of the raider.

2. An independent investment banker or other qualified expert should give an opinion about the adequacy of the price offered.

3. Outside legal counsel should present an opinion on antitrust, regulatory, and other legal issues.

On what grounds can the board of directors reject a tender offer? The general rule is that any ground is sufficient if in the board's business judgment such an offer will not serve the best interests of the shareholders. Martin Lipton goes on to list possible grounds for opposition:

1. The price is inadequate.

2. The offer is poorly timed, because financial and stock price factors are expected to improve in the future or are cyclically low.

3. The merger is illegal according to federal law, state laws, or other regulations.

4. There will be an adverse effect on employees, the environment, or other constituencies besides shareholders.

5. There is reason to believe the merger will not be consummated.

6. All shareholders will not be provided for equally.

7. In an exchange offer for the bidder's securities, the quality of those securities is in question.

Legal Challenges

Legal tactics are the first line of defense. In fact, defense strategy is typically the function of attorneys who have developed a specialty in takeover defense. The objective is generally twofold. The first is to find a legal impediment, called a "showstopper," that will prevent the proposed business combination. Generally, the most effective showstoppers have been based on antitrust laws. Should one of the two federal agencies with antitrust jurisdiction declare a proposed business combination to be in violation of federal law and institute an action, there is a strong possibility that the takeover will be blocked. There are few other legal tactics that can have this dramatic effect. The second objective of the legal defense is to delay the tender offer long enough to discourage and deter the acquirer or to enable the target company to find a friendly white knight to intercede. Such delays also can have the effect of pushing bids higher in an effort to win over recalcitrant management.

The elemental strategy of most legal defenses is quite straightforward. The defending company will try to raise as many legal issues in federal and state courts as well as regulatory agencies as possible. If the target company prevails on only one issue in only one of these courts or agencies, it may still win the temporary injunction that will provide it time to take the other steps in its defense plan.

While the demonstration of antitrust violations is generally the most effective defense tactic, challenges to the acquiring company over disclosure requirements under the Williams Act have in the past periodically proved successful for delay. Allegations of margin violations, which are complex borrowing rules for financing stock, also may be effective, although corporations now are careful to adhere to the law in this area. Similarly, although the validity of state takeover laws is now under attack, a number of challenges can be raised in various states under state fiduciary standards. But first let's summarize the basic federal challenges.

Disclosure Rules

The Securities and Exchange Commission has adopted a number of disclosure rules under the Williams Act. These requirements provide two general areas of potential violations. In Schedule 14(d)(1), the corporate acquirer must disclose specified information. The defending company can challenge any one of these disclosures as materially incomplete or incorrect.

Martin Lipton suggests some of the grounds on which disclosure violations can be charged:

1. The purpose of the offer.
2. The financing of the offer.
3. Prior contacts with management or directors of the target company.

4. The impact of regulatory requirements.
5. Unreported misconduct or violation of law.

One of the potential benefits of such challenges is that information may be discovered in court proceedings that could be damaging to the raiding company. But generally disclosure violations will not be showstoppers. Such violations usually can be corrected easily, sometimes without the need for injunctive relief. Nevertheless, numerous challenges can win effective delays.

Conflicts of Interest

Commercial banks provide the financing for tender offers. But because there are relatively few banks of sufficient size and expertise to finance large takeovers, they often have overlapping clients. This leads to potential charges of misuse of confidential information about one client in favor of another.

However, these charges have not been effective in stopping mergers. Commercial and investment banks are aware of their potential vulnerability in this regard. Therefore, they have developed careful controls, dubbed Chinese walls, to separate the functions of their firms. These controls have proved to be effective in deflecting legal challenges over conflicts of interest and misuse of confidential information.

Margin Requirements

The method of financing a tender offer sometimes has provided grounds for actionable court challenges against a raider. Typically, an acquiring company will borrow sizable funds from a commercial bank. These borrowings fall under the Federal Reserve Board's margin requirements, which can be complex. A key part of these rules restricts the amount of funds that can be borrowed against margin securities.

Another restricts investment bankers, especially broker-dealers, from arranging financing. Failure to meet the letter of these regulations can result in injunctive relief.

But generally, these violations can be corrected quickly. Moreover, financial institutions are now more sensitive to such requirements and more careful to meet them. Finally, a recent amendment to the margin rules liberalized some of the requirements, including the assets which may be used to provide collateral for a loan.

Antitrust Laws

Antitrust law, of course, is a large body of study unto itself. The Hart-Scott-Rodino Act, as previously noted, requires that notice be given to the Federal Trade Commission and the Justice Department, the antitrust agencies, to allow them to take action. A refusal to take action, however, does not constitute approval of a merger. Nor will it necessarily deter a target company from bringing action on antitrust grounds in federal court.

The major federal antitrust statutes are the Clayton Act, Section 7 of which allows the blocking of a merger if it is found to reduce competition or create a monopoly, and the Sherman Act, which prohibits a business combination if it is found to restrain interstate commerce or foreign trade. The most common ground for an antitrust violation under the Clayton Act is the so-called horizontal merger in which two direct competitors who do business in the same "market" are combined. As Martin Lipton and Henry Lesser point out, the following are other grounds for finding antitrust violations.

1. A merger, in which a supplier or customer is acquired.
2. The acquisition of a company that is a potential com-

petitor in the same product and geographical area. This is a recent argument, and so far has proved to be of little avail.

3. An acquisition that will enable a well-entrenched company to prevent competition because of its access to the resources of the acquired company.

There also has been a movement in Congress to pass legislation against so-called conglomerate mergers essentially on the basis of size alone. That movement so far has floundered.

In practice, the corporate raider will make its own antitrust determinations. Often, the corporation will prepare plans to sell a division that might be construed as anticompetitive if combined with the target company. The Justice Department has expressed its sympathy toward permitting a raider to divest itself of the tainted assets and allowing the bid to proceed on this basis. This policy undercuts any target's defense position.

The most successful showstoppers have involved the horizontal-merger argument. One of the best examples of a successful showstopper arose in the contest between LTV Corporation and Grumman Corporation in 1981. Grumman made a successful enough antitrust case to win a preliminary injunction against the merger. LTV then dropped its offer.

Financial and Structural Defense Tactics

If legal objections are the first line of defense, financial and structural changes in a target company are the most dramatic methods of defending a corporation against a proposed takeover. These changes may include acquisitions, liquidations, spin-offs, self-tenders, and so-called Pac-Man defenses that might stop an acquirer. Each of these defenses is discussed below.

Acquisitions

There are several objectives for acquisitions by the target company:

1. *To create an antitrust conflict.* As we have noted in a pre-bid situation, a target company can still seek now to acquire another company that would put it in direct competition with the raider, making it subject to the antitrust laws.

2. *To create a regulatory conflict.* An acquisition of a company in a federally regulated business will at least delay a merger until the necessary approvals are won. It also can provide obstacles because the raiding company may not qualify or may not be allowed to own a company in the industry. Once again, however, the raider can agree to put such assets into a trust, pending approval or divestment.

3. *To utilize attractive financial assets.* A target company can make an acquisition in order to reduce its cash or increase its debt. The goal here is to reduce the target company's financial assets—assets which are its principal attractiveness to the corporate raider.

Sale of Business

In some cases, a corporate acquirer is principally interested in a specific business or asset, such as a natural resource, that is owned by the target company. The company can sell that business or asset, often called the "crown jewel," thus reducing its attractiveness to the would-be buyer.

There have been many examples of this strategy. In the face of a hostile bid from Limited, Inc., in 1984 Carter Hawley Hale gave General Cinema Corporation an option to buy its most successful property, Waldenbooks. Along with other tactics, the option helped to defeat the hostile bid.

Partial Liquidations and Spin-offs

In a strategy related to the one above, a target company can sell an undervalued business or undervalued assets for the going market value and distribute the proceeds to the stockholders. This is called a partial liquidation.

The undervalued business also can be sold in what has come to be termed a spin-off. In a spin-off, the shareholders usually are given shares in the spun-off venture so that they retain their interest. The sale is then not subject to the risk of not getting top price in the rush to sell. Also, unlike a liquidation distributed in cash, which is taxable to the stockholders, securities are generally tax-free.

Self-Tender

In response to a tender offer, a target company may choose to tender for a portion of its own shares at a higher price than is being offered by the raiding company. This is especially attractive to a cash-rich company.

The Carter Hawley Hale defense is again a good example. The company bought up more than 50 percent of its shares in the open market. This was not an official tender but accomplished the same purpose. Coupled with the stock sold to General Cinema, Carter Hawley Hale management was able to almost gain majority control of the remaining shares of the company.

Complete Liquidation

A company, especially one rich in undervalued assets, may choose to liquidate entirely rather than accept the acquiring company's bid. This is an option if the total values are substantially in excess of the bidder's offering price and shareholders can be convinced to wait the few months required to implement the plan. In 1980, UV Industries was able to defeat a hostile bid from Victor Posner (through Sharon Steel Corporation) by liquidating itself.

Leveraged Buy-out

Management may be able to buy its own company through a leveraged buy-out. In a leveraged buy-out banks and insurance companies provide debt financing based on the company's cash flow and assets in order to buy the company.

In the 1984 battle for Gulf Oil Corporation, which would become the largest takeover of all time, one competing bid was a leveraged buy-out that involved management. That alternative lost to a very strong bid from Standard Oil of California. In 1984, many leveraged buy-outs were successfully completed, such as Amerace Corporation, American Sterilizer Company, and Dr. Pepper Company.

Poison Pill

In 1983 Brown-Forman Distillers Corporation made a hostile bid for Lennox Industries. Brown-Forman was a family-controlled company. Within a couple of weeks of the initial offer, Lennox declared a dividend that consisted of a new issue of convertible preferred stock. If a merger occurred, the preferred stock would become convertible into voting stock of the remaining entity. This is what is known as a "poison pill." In other words, if Brown-Forman succeeded in taking over Lennox, the Lennox shareholders would be able to convert their shares into voting shares in Brown-Forman. That would dilute the Brown family's control. By taking over Lennox—and by being compelled to swallow the poison pill—the Browns would lose some control. In this case, Brown-Forman swallowed hard and won the company, paying a higher price to avoid having to digest the poison pill.

Raising Dividends

A cash-rich company may choose to reduce its attractiveness to a raider and increase support among shareholders by raising dividends or declaring a special dividend.

Tender Offer for the Raider: The Pac-Man Defense

A few companies have countered a tender offer by making their own tender offer for the raiding company. This has proved a better tactic for creating delays and confusion than actually deterring the bid or taking over the raiding company. Martin Marietta Corporation, for example, took this stance successfully in what was then dubbed the "Pac-Man defense" (after the popular video game in which gobbling up one's opponent is the best way to survive), against Bendix Corporation in 1982. Bendix ultimately had to sell out to Allied Corporation.

Similarly, in 1984, Houston Natural Gas Corporation, as one of many moves in its defense against Coastal Corporation's hostile bid, tendered for Coastal. Ultimately, Houston Natural won and retained its independence. In the cases of both Marietta and Houston, the defense would have so disabled the companies, because of the accumulated debt, that a takeover would have lost considerable value. Such extreme defensive tactics have become known as "scorched earth" policies.

Ad Hoc Techniques

Target companies muster every possible method they can to fend off takeover bids. Labor unions, too, have become involved in the fight against hostile bidders. Vitriolic public attacks on the raiding management sometimes have worked to thwart takeover grabs. Some managers have even threatened to resign in the event a takeover succeeds. In the battle between Houston Natural and Coastal, Houston discovered an old agreement that Coastal had signed which prevented it from doing business with a Houston customer. The Texas attorney general then brought a suit against Coastal, which helped to stop the bid.

White Knights

The last line of defense for a target company is to search for a white knight, in the hope that that corporation will acquire the target company at a higher price and on more agreeable terms than the raiding company is offering. The danger, of course, is that once the white knight is invited in, it will become less accommodating. Astute target companies begin to search for such white knights immediately upon receiving a hostile tender offer. The short time that most tender offers are open makes this imperative. Some companies, as noted, will already have made overtures to potential third-party acquirers before any bid is made. Many investment bankers have compiled lists of potential white knights.

Probably the best-known early example of a white knight defense was the J. Ray McDermott takeover of Babcock and Wilcox. Under the able leadership of Harry Gray, Jr., United Technologies made a hostile bid for Babcock and Wilcox in early 1977. The takeover contest was then not nearly so well developed nor as large as it would eventually become. The much smaller J. Ray McDermott entered the fray a month later. The arbitrage community had not seen a bidding contest like it before. McDermott started making open-market purchases and then bid for the company. Babcock and Wilcox was at $34 when the bidding began. McDermott's winning bid was $65.

A chronology of events follows:

Case Study: Babcock and Wilcox, United Technologies, and J. Ray McDermott

Date	Action	NYSE Closing Prices Babcock and Wilcox	United Technol- ogies	McDermott
3/28/77		$34^3/_4$	$34^3/_4$	$50^1/_4$
3/29/77	United Technologies announces un-friendly tender offer. Terms: United Technologies offers $42 per share for Babcock and Wilcox's 12.6 million outstanding shares.	No trading	$34^1/_2$	$50^3/_4$
3/30/77		40	$34^3/_4$	$50^1/_2$
4/4/77	Babcock and Wilcox files complaint in Ohio, saying United Technologies' bid is grossly inadequate and alleging potential antitrust violations and criminal violations under the Atomic Energy Act.	$39^1/_2$	$34^1/_2$	$52^1/_2$
4/6/77	United Technologies submits an 041 Filing re: Ohio take-over statute and files with Nuclear Regulatory Commission (NRC).	$40^1/_2$	$34^5/_8$	$53^1/_4$

Date	Action	NYSE Closing Prices		
		Babcock and Wilcox	United Technologies	McDermott
4/8/77	Holiday. Babcock and Wilcox files request at NRC that emergency action be taken to halt tender offer.	—	—	—
4/14/77	Babcock and Wilcox says Ohio sets hearings on United Technologies tender. Ohio Division of Securities grants request of Babcock and Wilcox for hearing under Ohio takeover statute. Hearing set for 4/25/77 is pursuant to Ohio Commerce Department's legislated power to determine whether bid complies with state's 1969 takeover law.	40½	36¾	55
5/4/77	Babcock and Wilcox sues J. Ray McDermott over stock purchases in federal court in Akron, Ohio. Suit asks for injunction and charges violations of Ohio securities laws and federal Atomic Energy Act.	44	39⅛	55

Date	Action	NYSE Closing Prices		
		Babcock and Wilcox	United Technologies	McDermott
5/9/77	NRC denies Babcock and Wilcox's request for emergency halt of tender.	$43\frac{1}{2}$	$39\frac{5}{8}$	$52\frac{5}{8}$
5/10/77		$43\frac{3}{4}$	$40\frac{1}{2}$	53
5/11/77	J. Ray McDermott files Schedule 13(d) revealing ownership of more than 5% of Babcock and Wilcox shares. McDermott will not disclose number held.	$44\frac{1}{4}$	$40\frac{1}{4}$	53
5/12/77	McDermott holds 8.7% Babcock and Wilcox (1.1 million shares) as of 5/9. Reason given for purchase was to acquire minority interest but said it does not seek to control Babcock and Wilcox; however, it is prepared to explore possibility of a merger.	$44\frac{7}{8}$	$40\frac{1}{8}$	53
5/17/77	Briefs filed by Babcock and Wilcox say price and terms of United Technologies offer unfair and Canadian foreign investment and disclosure is incomplete.	$44\frac{7}{8}$	$40\frac{3}{8}$	56

Date	Action	NYSE Closing Prices		
		Babcock and Wilcox	United Technologies	McDermott
5/17/77 (Cont.)	United Technologies files brief in Akron in support of motion to dismiss Babcock and Wilcox complaint. Brief contains amendments to United Technologies' offering statement. United Technologies will extend duration of offer if court feels it is insufficient, and it will not oppose order to withdraw the offer because of pending litigation.	44⅞	40⅜	56
5/18/77		44¾	40⅜	56
5/19/77	McDermott owns 9.9% through 5/13/77.	43⅝	40⅜	55⅞
5/20/77	Babcock and Wilcox files request for hearing in New Jersey with New Jersey Bureau of Securities.	44⅛	40⅛	55⅞
5/23/77	Ohio Division of Securities hearing examiner report released in favor of United Technologies. Only change requested is that United Technologies	43½	39⅞	55

| | | NYSE Closing Prices | | |
| | | Babcock and Wilcox | United Technologies | |
Date	Action			McDermott
5/23/77 (Cont.)	hold offer open twenty days and not original ten-day period.	43$^{1/2}$	39$^{7/8}$	55
5/24/77	Babcock and Wilcox file objection in United Technologies case. United Technologies files application under New Jersey and Arkansas takeover statutes for hearing on tender. Ohio Commerce Department legal counsel Wideman allows United Technologies to proceed with its tender following two weeks of hearings on the offer. Babcock and Wilcox will have ten days to submit responses to decision to state securities commissioner. Wideman's Commissioner James Hurd will probably respond by 6/3/77 to Wideman's recommendation to proceed with the tender offer.	44$^{3/8}$	39$^{3/8}$	54$^{5/8}$

Date	Action	NYSE Closing Prices		
		Babcock and Wilcox	United Technologies	McDermott
6/2/77	Motion filed by Babcock and Wilcox with District of Columbia Circuit Court for expedited appeal on NRC issue.	45$7/8$	37$7/8$	53
6/3/77	Ohio Securities Commissioner Hurd accepts Wideman's recommendation. Babcock and Wilcox requests that Arkansas securities commissioner amend his delay order, which originally ran for only thirty days, to run until all pending litigation is resolved.	45$7/8$	38$3/8$	54$3/8$
6/6/77	Babcock and Wilcox appeals Ohio Division of Securities decision that takeover could go forward. Appeal alleges inadequate disclosure information. Suit assigned to Judge Rader in Franklin County Common Pleas Court.	46$3/4$	38$1/8$	54$1/8$

Date	Action	NYSE Closing Prices		
		Babcock and Wilcox	United Technologies	McDermott
6/7/77	Babcock and Wilcox goes to Superior Court of New Jersey Appellate Division to file notice of accelerated appeal. New Jersey Supreme Court will consider Babcock and Wilcox and United Technologies' request for accelerated hearing on appeal.	45⅞	38¼	55
6/14/77	Arkansas hearing goes ahead with offer only after Ohio and New Jersey courts give go ahead.	—	—	—
6/16/77	Ohio Appellate Division denies United Technologies' motion to vacate stay order of hearing office—will be in effect until 6/19/77. New Jersey Supreme Court denies United Technologies' motion for leave to appeal the 6/7/77 order of the Appellate Division, which set hearing on the issue of discretion abuse for 8/8/77.	45¾	40¼	54⅝

| | | NYSE Closing Prices | | |
		Babcock and Wilcox	United Technol- ogies	McDermott
Date	Action			
7/5/77	U.S. Justice Depart- ment moves to block United Tech- nologies–Babcock and Wilcox merger. It files civil antitrust suit, stating merger would eliminate competition in man- ufacture and sale of generating equip- ment used for elec- tric production. Suit filed in U.S. District Court in Hartford, Connecticut, where United Technologies is based. Suit asks that any acquisition be declared illegal and United Technol- ogies be prevented from acquiring any Babcock and Wilcox stock.	43$\frac{5}{8}$	41	58$\frac{1}{4}$
7/7/77	Motion filed by United Technologies in federal court in Hartford to transfer matter to Ohio Fed- eral District Court.	42$\frac{3}{8}$	41	58
7/18/77	A federal court de- nies the request for court order blocking the United	45	39$\frac{7}{8}$	55$\frac{1}{4}$

Date	Action	NYSE Closing Prices		
		Babcock and Wilcox	United Technol- ogies	McDermott
7/18/77 (Cont.)	Technologies tender offer.	45	39⅞	55¼
8/5/77	United Technologies increases its tender offer to $48 per share.	47⅛	38⅞	52
8/16/77	Babcock's board recommends to shareholders the J. Ray McDermott tender offer made 8/14 of $55 per share for 4.3 million shares (35% of the outstanding), to be followed up with merger negotiations.	51⅝	37	52
8/19/77	United Technologies raises its tender offer to $55 per share for all of the outstanding shares.	57	35⅞	51
8/22/77	McDermott increases its tender offer to $60 for 4.3 million shares. The tender offer will be followed up with a merger in which shareholders will receive an unspecified package of securities of comparable value, $60 per share.	56⅜	35½	51⅝

Date	Action	*NYSE Closing Prices*		
		Babcock and Wilcox	*United Technol- ogies*	*McDermott*
8/24/77	United Technologies raises its tender offer for all out-standing shares to $58.50 per share. McDermott raises its offer to $62.50 for 4.3 million shares with a subse-quent tax-free com-bination for an unspecified package of securities of com-parable value to fol-low.	57³/₈	35⁵/₈	52
8/25/77	Babcock declares a $2.50 special divi-dend in an attempt to bolster the Mc-Dermott tender offer of 8/24/77. United Technologies counters by offering to pay 50% of the special dividend to holders whose shares were tendered under its $58.50-per-share offer.	58³/₈	35¹/₂	49
9/7/77	McDermott receives 9.1 million shares in its $62.50-per-share tender offer for 4.3 million shares.	59³/₄	37¹/₂	48⁵/₈

		NYSE Closing Prices		
Date	Action	Babcock and Wilcox	United Technologies	McDermott
12/8/77	McDermott resumes talks with Babcock and Wilcox's board regarding the tax-free swap of securities for the remaining 51%, which McDermott has not yet acquired.	58	$35^{3}/_{4}$	$53^{7}/_{8}$
12/9/77	McDermott and Babcock and Wilcox agree to the terms of the securities to be exchanged for each remaining share of latter: one share of $2.50 nonconvertible cumulative preferred stock and one share of $2.20 convertible accumulative preferred stock of McDermott. Each preferred share would have a liquidation value of $31.25, giving the package a liquidation value of $62.50 per share.	$57^{1}/_{4}$	$36^{3}/_{4}$	$54^{7}/_{8}$
1/31/78	Babcock and Wilcox and McDermott schedules shareholder meetings for 3/30/78 to approve the merger.	$57^{1}/_{2}$	34	$49^{1}/_{2}$

Date	Action	NYSE Closing Prices		
		Babcock and Wilcox	United Technol- ogies	McDermott
2/22/78	McDermott and Babcock and Wilcox announce slightly better terms. The $2.50 nonconvertible preferred is improved to $2.60 nonconvertible preferred.	58¼	33⅞	48½
3/30/78	The shareholders of both McDermott and Babcock and Wilcox approve the merger.	59⅜	35⅞	47½

Lock-up Agreements

In the early 1980s, a financial technique that came to be known as a "lock-up" was utilized to give white knights an advantage over the initial corporate raider. The target company would arrange a stock-purchase or stock-option agreement with the white knight, usually selling or giving the white knight the option to buy up a large portion of the target. In the event a hostile bidder sought to take over the company, that bidder might have to contend with the white knight as a minority shareholder or be compelled to pay more to acquire the entire target company. Should the acquiring company succeed, the white knight retains the option to buy in. The objective of the lock-up agreement is to deter other bidders.

But several lock-up agreements have been challenged by the federal courts. In one particularly interesting case, the lock-up agreement made between Marathon Oil and U.S. Steel (the white knight brought in to fend off Mobil Oil's bid for Marathon) was found to be manipulative. Legal and financial experts were surprised by the ruling. Marathon had granted U.S. Steel a stock option to buy a substantial block of Marathon shares. U.S. Steel also would have the right to purchase Marathon's Yates oil field interests, its crown jewel, should another party succeed in taking over Marathon.

Most attorneys believe there is still room for forms of lock-up agreements. The lock-up technique has since been used in such takeover defenses as that of the St. Regis Corporation against Rupert Murdoch and the Continental Group against Sir James Goldsmith.

Legal Questions in Defending Corporations

The legal status of defense strategies is always subject to challenge and change. Thus, no book can pronounce the final word on such strategies. But the overriding legal principle on which most aspects of defense are based is known as the business judgment rule. Over the years, a large body of case law has developed in support of this rule. In 1981 the federal court in the Northern District of Illinois in *Panter* v. *Marshall Field & Co.* interpreted this rule. It serves as a good definition of the principle (this decision was upheld by the Seventh Circuit Court of Appeals):

> [D]irectors of corporations discharge their fiduciary duties when in good faith they exercise business judgment in making decisions regarding the corporation. When they act in good faith, they enjoy a presumption of sound business judgment, reposed in them as directors, which courts will not disturb if any rational business purpose can be attributed to their decisions. In the absence of fraud, bad faith, gross over-reaching or abuse of discretion, courts will

not interfere with the exercise of business judgment
by corporate directors.

Many conventional defense tactics have been supported
by the courts on the basis of the business judgment rule.
The initial response of directors trying to fend off a takeover
has been protected by this rule. According to most legal
experts, directors may reasonably reject a tender offer without fear of legal liability. But directors also must make an
effort to make a fair appraisal of the offer and to evaluate
its financial aspects. It is prudent to do so based on independent outside advice.

Widespread judicial acceptance of the business judgment
rule has placed the burden of proof on a plaintiff, who must
show that directors have acted in bad faith. The courts assume that corporate directors are acting in good faith unless
otherwise proven. Courts do not consider themselves ca-
pable of making business decisions. That is the essential
ground on which the business judgment rule rests. As the
Court of Appeals in the Second Circuit ruled in 1980 in the
case of *Crouse-Hinds Corp.* v. *Internorth*:

> It appears to us that the business judgment doctrine,
> at least in part, is grounded in the prudent recogni-
> tion that courts are ill-equipped and infrequently called
> on to evaluate what are and must be essentially busi-
> ness judgments. The authority and responsibilities
> vested in corporate directors both by statute and de-
> cisional law proceed on the assumption that ines-
> capably there can be no available objective standard
> by which the correctness of every corporate decision
> may be measured, by the courts or otherwise. Even
> if that were not the case, by definition the respon-
> sibility for business judgments must rest with the
> corporate directors; their individual capabilities and

experience peculiarly qualify them for the discharge
of that responsibility.

Summary

Takeover defenses can begin long before an offer for the
company is made. Such pre-bid defenses include charter provisions that require a supermajority of shareholders to vote
approval of a merger, as well as other measures such as
staggering the election of directors and voting special compensation to management in the event of a takeover.

Once a bid is made, the best defense is an antitrust action
supported by the Federal Trade Commission or the Justice
Department. Such legal barriers to a merger are known as
showstoppers. But other defenses have worked too. Corporations can sell their most valuable property, acquire a
company themselves (thus deepening their debt), or even
bid for the bidder itself. In many instances, the defense is
as aggressive as the offense. The arbitrageur must understand which defenses can work and where and when companies are most vulnerable.

8
OTHER ARBITRAGE
OPPORTUNITIES AND
SPECIAL SITUATIONS

Professional arbitrageurs do not generally restrict themselves to merger arbitrage alone. There are many other opportunities to engage in arbitrage that arise from securities offerings, corporate reorganizations, and liquidations. Similarly, there are new trading devices that aid conventional risk arbitrage. This chapter provides a concise, technical summary of these arbitrage activities.

Convertible Securities

Convertible securities, including both bonds and preferred stock, generally provide the holder with an option to convert the security into the corporation's common stock. These conversions are for a specified number of shares, at a particular price, and for a limited time period. Convertible preferred stock or debentures carry a dividend or interest as well. The market generally puts a premium on securities. For example, a $1,000 bond that is convertible into 50 shares of common stock at $20 per share often will trade for more than its face value of $1,000. When the price of the stock changes, the price of the convertible security changes along with it. This permits holders of, say, the bond to enjoy both annual income from interest and to participate in the growth of the company. Convertibles also have lower margin requirements than either common or preferred stock. But some convertible bonds have call provisions that allow the corporation to buy back bonds if interest rates fall below a specific level. Conversion could be forced if the selling price of the bond exceeds the call price.

The value of the shares specified in a convertible security is known as the parity value. Convertibles, as noted above, usually sell at a premium to their parity value since they yield more income than the common stock in the form of interest. They often have other credit characteristics as well. For example, if the price of the underlying stock goes up, then the parity value of the bond increases while the premium of the convertible tends to shrink. If the common stock rises enough, the convertible will often lose much of its premium and sell closer to its parity value. It is at this point that a nearly pure arbitrage opportunity appears. The reason is that the convertible is almost a direct proxy for the common shares. The arbitrageur's strategy is to buy the convertible close to parity and sell short the common shares into which it is convertible. There is little risk of loss in such a transaction. If the common stock goes up, the convertible can be converted into the common stock and used to cover the short position. If the common stock drops in price, the convertible often starts to regain some of its premium and thus won't fall as far. Engaging in an act of arbitrage in such a situation means that the loss on the convertible is less than the gain on the common stock by the amount of the premium. The arbitrageur has, in effect, created a free put on the underlying common stock. Here is an example of convertible arbitrage:

On January 30, 1984, the Financial Corporation of America's common stock closed at 23. The Financial Corporation 11½s of 2002 (convertible into 68.17 shares of common) closed at 153. The conversion value of the bond is 68.17 × 23 = 1567.91. Thus, the bond closed at a $38 discount to its conversion value. One can set up an arbitrage position by purchasing bonds and selling short 68 shares per bond, at the above prices, locking in the $38 profit. This profit could be realized by converting the bond into common.

Alternatively, the long-bond, short-stock position could be held in the expectation that the stock price will decline. The convertible would then typically trade at a larger premium. By August 20, the common was trading at 6 while the bonds had declined to 62¼. Here the parity value of the bond (the conversion value at $6 a share) is 41 and the premium is 21¼.

The profit on the arbitrage now can be computed as follows:

Bond	$(0.622.50 - 1.530.0) \times 1000$	=	(907.50)
Stock	$68.17 \times (23 - 6)$	=	1158.89
Net profit			251.39

The net profit also is equal to the discount ($37.91) on setting up the position plus the premium ($213.48) on the bond when the position is unwound.

Spin-offs

When a company forms a new corporate entity for, say, a division or subsidiary, and distributes the new entity's stock to its shareholders, it is called a spin-off. Spin-offs can involve partial distributions as well. Shareholders retain their original stock and receive new stock of one or more of a company's subsidiaries. The stock usually will be sold on a when-issued basis. If the spin-off satisfies federal and state tax requirements, the shares are distributed tax-free to the recipient. If the tax code's requirements are not wholly met, the distribution is treated as a dividend.

Spin-off Arbitrage

Let's say that a company decides to spin off a subsidiary to its shareholders. Once the proposal has been approved by the Securities and Exchange Commission, the stock of the subsidiary can be traded on a when-issued basis on the New York Stock Exchange. Payment for such shares is not due until the record date of the spin-off. The company's own stock (minus the spin-off) also will trade when-issued.

These three securities should trade in a constant relationship to each other. The price of the regular way common stock plus the interest cost to carry the stock until record date should be equal to the price of the spin-off when-issued plus the price of the company's common stock ex-spin-off when-issued. When this relationship is violated, there is a potential opportunity for arbitrage. If the regular way security sells at a discount greater than the interest expense, the arbitrageur will buy the regular way security, and sell short the when-issued securities, thus locking in the difference. If the regular way security sells at a premium to the when-issued securities, the arbitrageur will buy the when-issued securities and sell short the regular way common stock. Note that a NYSE member firm receives a partial interest income on the short sale of common stock.

Here is an example of spin-off arbitrage:

On December 28, 1982, Mesa Petroleum spun off one unit of beneficial interest in Mesa Offshore Trust for each common share of Mesa. The when-issued shares started trading on December 13. The closing prices were as follows:

Mesa (regular way)	14.375
(Interest cost to carry for fifteen days)	+.060
	14.435
Mesa ex-spin-off (when-issued)	12.50
Mesa Offshore (when-issued)	+2.25
	14.75

The common closed at a discount to the when-issued securities. One can establish the arbitrage position by buying the common at 14.375 and selling the two when-issued securities short at a total price of 14.75. The .375 profit on the transaction would be reduced by the 6-cents-per-share cost to hold the position until the ex-date. At that point, the spin-off is used to cover the short Mesa Offshore when-issued and the common stock ex-spin-off is delivered against the when-issued ex-spin-off position.

Stubs

Stubs are essentially cash or stock distributions, or payouts, that arise from a merger between two corporate entities. After the legal closing of a merger, there is often potential for such financial distributions in addition to the immediate payout terms of the merger deal. These distributions can take the form of "certificates of contingent interest," or rights to marketable units of a company which are generally traded on a when-issued basis. These rights, or stubs, must be analyzed to gauge their current and estimated future value. Since the stubs represent a unit of interest in a trust that will own certain properties and operations of a company's subsidiary operations, they are subject to the same kind of technical and fundamental analysis as the valuation of a company's common stock as a whole. This includes a thorough analysis of the unit's earnings' potential and its estimated price-earnings multiple, which generally reflects the Wall Street community's consensus of what the trading level of the unit should be. The trading value is a function of the unit's estimated earnings times its estimated multiple.

Pure stubs are residual values representing the properties and liabilities left in a company following the liquidation of most of its assets and distribution of the proceeds to shareholders. As such, pure stub situations are relatively rare. Nevertheless, one such example was the liquidation of Arcata Corporation in 1982. The company sold most of its assets and distributed the net proceeds, after payment of liabilities and debt, to its shareholders. Prior to the liquidation, Arcata traded at about $29 per share. The net proceeds distributed to shareholders were about $28.50. Current owners of the Arcata stubs who purchased Arcata just before its liquidation owned the stock at a net cost of around $.50 per share. In the late summer of 1983 the stub was trading in the market at about $3.75 per share. The buyer before the liquidation received cash of $28.50 plus a security valued at $3.75 by the end of 1983.

Spin-offs from Partial Liquidation

American General Corporation's takeover in January of 1984 of Gulf United Corporation for $1.1 billion in stocks and warrants is a good example. The terms of the deal included a spin-off of Gulf United's Gulf Broadcasting unit (which represented about 20 percent of the company's book value), payable to Gulf shareholders in the form of common stock. Each Gulf share also would be exchanged for one-half share of a new series of American General cumulative convertible preferred stock, with a $46 stated value and paying annual dividends of $2.64. Also included was one fourth of a five-year warrant to buy American General common, exercisable at the higher of either $23.50 or the average trading price of American General common for a specified pricing period. American General's new preferred shares were convertible into American General common on a one-for-one basis. The estimated trading value of the broadcasting spin-off would be about $6 per share.

If the arbitrageur values the preferred stock at $42.50 and the warrant at $7 (both vary, reflecting the market value of American General common), the total deal value would be $29 (i.e., one half of the preferred, or $21.25, one fourth of the warrant, or $1.75, and the stub, valued at $6).

Options

Options are financial contracts that give the holder the right to either buy or sell an underlying security at a particular price for a specified time period. A call option gives the holder the right to buy an underlying security while a put option gives the holder the right to sell a security. An option writer, or seller, is obliged to perform according to the terms of the option, delivering calls or purchasing puts of 100-share lots of a particular stock, if and when they are exercised.

The exercise, or striking, price is directly related to the price at which a buyer can purchase the underlying security of a call or sell the underlying security of a put. For example, an XYZ June 20 *call* gives the option buyer the right to purchase 100 shares of XYZ stock at $20 per share until the third Friday in June. An XYZ June 20 *put* gives the option buyer the right to sell 100 shares of XYZ stock at $20 per share regardless of the current market price of the stock. If either the put or call described above has not been exercised prior to the option's expiration date, the option ceases to exist or have any value.

An option has intrinsic value when the stock's current market value is above the option's strike price, in the case of a call, or below it, in the case of a put. For example, the XYZ June 20 call would have had an intrinsic value of $5 per share if the current market price of the stock was $25. This particular call option is said to be "in the money" by $5. If the XYZ stock's market price dropped to $20 per share, the call would be "at the money." It would be "out of the money" if the stock fell below $20.

At-the-money and out-of-the-money options have no intrinsic value but still might command a premium for their time value. Time value consists of whatever investors would pay for an option over intrinsic value in the hope that it would gain value prior to expiration because of a change in the price of the stock. At-the-money or out-of-the-money options usually trade on time value, although time value often can be an added factor in raising the premiums of in-the-money options. Listed common stock options expire on the Saturday following the third Friday of the expiration month. An option buyer pays the option seller a premium for the rights conveyed by the option. Premium values fluctuate widely in response to such factors as the relationship between the option and price of the underlying security, the volatility of that security, the time remaining before an option expires, and economic factors such as interest rates.

Options give investors the benefits of leverage and limited risk. A call option on 100 shares of, say, IBM gives the option holder the opportunity to control many times the number of shares he could otherwise buy for the same money. The dollar risk is limited to the premium (or price) of the option. But the investor holds his interest only until the expiration date.

History and Development
Option trading in the over-the-counter markets has been in existence for many years, but it was not until the establishment of regulated exchanges in the mid-1970s that the

practice grew widespread. The main options exchanges are the Chicago Board Options Exchange (CBOE), the American Stock Exchange (AMEX), the Pacific Stock Exchange, and the Philadelphia Stock Exchange. The Options Clearing Corporation acts as a central clearinghouse, and is regulated, like the exchanges, by the Securities and Exchange Commission.

Most options positions are closed out with an offsetting purchase or sale before they are exercised, even though they may be exercised at any time prior to their expiration date. The expiration date and exercise price of an option are set by the exchange. Common-stock options come in three-month intervals with three different expiration months, i.e., an XYZ call could have September, December, and March expiration dates. A new call, which expires in nine months, is opened when each series expires.

Arbitrage Opportunities in Option Trading

There are a variety of option-trading strategies available to an individual investor that are beyond the scope of this book. Trading opportunities for arbitrageurs are created through hedging techniques that approximate arbitrage situations. Hedging involves the taking of a position in a second transaction to reduce risk in the first.

Classic option hedges include simultaneous purchase of a call option to limit the risk of a short-stock sale. In this case, if the stock should rise, the loss would be limited to the price of the call option plus exercise price less short sale price. The reason: exercise of the call enables the short seller to cover his position at the call exercise price. One could also use a put to protect a shareholder's paper profit and insure against possible near-term losses. This is especially useful if a potential merger falls through. The put protects the holder against a stock price decline below this strike price.

A covered call writer (one who owns the underlying stock) is partially protected against loss because of the call premium income received. He also could collect premium profits on stocks that remain essentially unchanged in price.

Options Arbitrage

Options can provide arbitrage opportunities as they approach expiration. An example follows.

In-the-money options often sell at a discount to their intrinsic value as expiration nears. An arbitrage tactic would be to buy the option, sell the underlying stock, and exercise the option, thus making a profit on the point spread between the two. For example, as an XYZ April 20 call option approaches expiration, the market price of the stock reaches $24 per share. An arbitrageur bids $3\frac{3}{4}$ for the April 20 call, to which the public option holder responds. The arbitrageur then sells the common stock at $24, exercises his call, and makes a $\frac{1}{4}$-point profit. Alternatively, he could have sold the stock short and remained long with the call. At the same time there could be a $\frac{1}{8}$ bid for April 20 puts. The arbitrageur could then sell the put at $\frac{1}{8}$ against his previously held position, creating a total profit of $\frac{3}{8}$ point with no market risk. This is known as reverse conversion arbitrage. It is not recommended for the individual investor because the professional trader usually pays lower commissions and has sophisticated trading capability.

Dividend arbitrage occurs with an option whose underlying stock carries a large dividend. It makes sense to exercise a call option early on a high-dividend-paying stock, but this may be too costly for an individual investor. Arbitrageurs try to establish positions with little market risk, where they can exercise an option and receive a dividend.

For example, suppose XYZ stock sells at $28 per share. As its April option expiration date nears, a 50-cent dividend is due. An arbitrageur will buy April 20 calls at 8 and sell April 25 calls for 3, investing a total of $5 per share. On the day before the ex-dividend date, he will exercise the April 20 call and his position becomes long 100 shares of XYZ at $28 and short the April 25 call option at 3. He would earn $.50 on a $20 investment and will deliver the common shares against the April 25 call upon expiration.

Options in Merger Arbitrage

Options can be especially useful in classic merger-arbitrage transactions, in lieu of buying a stock long or selling short. Obviously, an arbitrageur has the choice of buying puts or selling calls rather than short-selling outright. The options can improve spreads and reduce capital costs, but a sophisticated analysis must be taken every time.

The following example of a merger-arbitrage transaction using options illustrates their value in improving one's spread.

Pfizer agreed to acquire Valleylab in November 1982. Holders of Valleylab would receive 0.448 share of Pfizer for each share owned. On November 15, Valleylab closed at 31 and Pfizer closed at $70^7/_8$. The spread was $^3/_4$ of a point (0.448 × $70^7/_8$ = 31.75). The spread could be increased by selling Pfizer December 70 call options, which were trading around 4 at that time. This is similar to a short sale of common stock at 74. On December expiration, Pfizer closed at $69^1/_8$ and the expired call options were worthless. The gain on the short-stock sale was $1^3/_4$ points ($70^7/_8$ − $69^1/_8$). The gain on the call option sale was the full 4 points. The call options, in this case, allowed the arbitrageur to increase the spread on the deal from $^3/_4$ to $1^3/_4$.

Here's an important point: the call-option strategy is superior to short-stock strategy *except* when the underlying stock drops by more than the price of the call option. In the example, had Pfizer fallen below $66^7/_8$, the call option would not have provided adequate protection against possible loss and shorting common stock would then be the best strategy. The arbitrageur must judge the likelihood of this occurring.

Interest-Rate Futures

To the uninitiated, mention of the futures market brings to mind a chaotic scene of shouting, handwringing commodity traders buying and selling contracts on such items as pork bellies and corn. While organized futures markets for commodity items have existed since the nineteenth century, the futures markets for financial instruments have been in place only since 1975. Commodity futures markets arose to meet the needs of commodity producers, merchants, processors, and creditors as a protection against fluctuating prices. A forward contract can involve any asset that can be traded for future delivery between two parties on mutually agreeable terms. A forward contract becomes a futures contract when the deal involves a standardized amount of a particular asset with specific delivery dates. Futures contracts provide a means of risk management by locking in the price of a particular item for the length of the contract. (Financial futures are contracts for the future delivery of financial instruments such as Treasury bonds, GNMAs, and certificates of deposit.)

The degree of volatility in interest rates is a recent phenomenon, since both short and long rates generally stayed within a 2- to 6-percent trading range for the twenty-five-year period following World War II. In the 1970s, high inflation rates and economic dislocations created a credit crunch and record-high interest rates on both short- and long-term debt.

The effective hedging of interest-rate risks has become a necessity for investment managers and underwriters anxious to increase their returns. It also opened the door for myriad forms of trading that are useful to arbitrageurs.

A historical summary of short- and long-term interest rates illustrates why these futures arose and retained their popularity as a means of reducing the risk of loss from rate swings. In early 1969, ninety-day Treasury bills and prime commercial paper averaged a 6.13-percent and 6.14-percent yield, respectively, up from 2.5 percent in 1960. Subsequently, they experienced two complete cycles of decline and recovery closing at a record 9-percent level at the end of 1978. Over the same period, long-term Treasury bonds traded at prices that offered yields of 4 percent to 4.25 percent in the early sixties, jumped to 6 percent in 1969 and a record-breaking 7 percent in mid-1970, and rose to an unheard-of 8.75 percent in 1978.

More recently, rates reached new highs with ninety-day Treasury bills reaching 16½ percent and long-term Treasury bonds yielding 15 percent in the summer of 1981.

The following table is a thirteen-year summary of short- and long-term Treasury rates using three-month Treasury bills. Hedgers in interest-rate futures had much to gain during the wide rate swings that began in 1980.

The main commodity exchanges in the United States and Canada are the Chicago Board of Trade, the Kansas City Board of Trade, the Chicago Mercantile Exchange, the New York Coffee, Sugar and Cocoa Exchange, the New York Cotton Exchange, the New York Mercantile Exchange, the Commodity Exchange New York (COMEX), the New York Futures Exchange, the International Monetary Market of the Chicago Mercantile Exchange (IMM), the Minneapolis Grain Exchange, and the Winnipeg Commodity Exchange.

The Chicago Board of Trade and the IMM pioneered the concept of interest-rate futures and remain the most important market. The shift away from traditional commodity trading occurred in 1972, when the IMM was established to provide an exchange for the trading of futures contracts on

3-MONTH
U.S. TREASURY BILLS

International Monetary Market
Weekly High, Low-Friday Close
Nearest Futures Contract

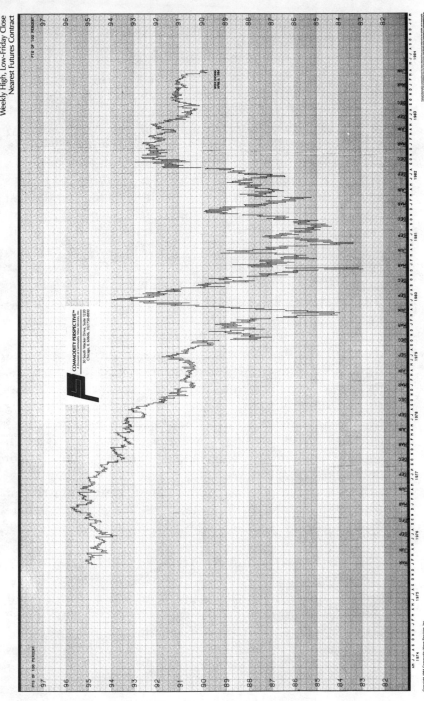

COMMODITY PERSPECTIVE™
a Division of Commodity News Services, Inc.
30 South Wacker Drive, Suite 1220
Chicago, IL 60606, 312/750-6840

WEEK ENDING
JUNE 8, 1984

14—TREASURY BILLS

silver coins and foreign currencies. Three years later, the Chicago Board of Trade established a market for Government National Mortgage Association (GNMA, commonly called Ginnie Maes) pass-through certificates. This was followed in 1976 by futures markets for three-month Treasury bills, and in 1978 by those for long-term Treasury bonds, ninety-day commercial paper, and one-year Treasury bills. Within two years after their inception, Treasury-bill futures and GNMA certificates became the fifth and fourteenth most active of the fifty-five futures contracts traded on the Chicago Mercantile Exchange. Today, trading in financial futures is also done on the New York Futures Exchange and commodity exchanges. The Commodity Futures Trading Commission, a federal agency with regulatory jurisdiction over the futures industry, reviews and approves applications for new contracts by exchanges.

In general, prices on financial futures contracts have been more volatile than price movements of underlying securities. As the delivery day of a futures contract approaches, its price converges toward the level of its cash counterpart since, with time running out, the room for wide-ranging expectation narrows. This relationship between futures prices and cash prices is called the basis and is a key issue in hedging transactions. Hedgers wish to eliminate the risk of unexpected price (interest-rate) changes by offsetting an existing long cash position with a short futures contract or vice versa. But the danger is that "the basis" can fluctuate unexpectedly.

Financial Futures in Merger Arbitrage

Arbitrageurs use various tactics to lock in the spread between similar or different futures contracts to earn a profit based on assessments of price discrepancies over time. These tactics involve the purchase of one futures contract and the sale of another in the hope that growing price differences between the two contracts will create a net profit. There are three basic types of spreads—intermonth, intermarket, and intercommodity. Intermonth spreads involve both long and short positions in two delivery months of the same contract; intermarket spreads are between similar futures contracts on different exchanges; and intercommodity spreads involve contracts for different maturities of similar securities.

Financial futures can effectively be used in merger arbitrage as well, especially when fixed-income securities are involved.

The U.S. Steel–Marathon Oil merger of 1981 offers an instance where trading in Treasury bond futures would have meant the difference between a profit and loss in a two-step tender offer deal.

In November 1981, U.S. Steel offered $125 per share for 51 percent of the Marathon Oil shares and fixed-income securities worth about $83 at the same time for the balance. The blended value of the deal was about $107 per Marathon share ([0.57 × 125] + [0.43 × 83]).

After the offer was announced and prior to the proration date, Marathon traded in a range from 99 to $107\frac{1}{4}$; thus the deal could have been set up at spreads ranging from 8 to $-\frac{1}{4}$ points. Assume that the average spread was 4 points. If the fixed-income securities fell in value by 9 points before they could be sold (about three months), the average profit before interest expense on the deal would evaporate. Bonds can easily fall 9 points in three months. In fact, after the proration date Marathon Oil sold at $71\frac{3}{8}$ on January 26, 1982, $11\frac{5}{8}$ points below the bond's value when the offer was announced.

In order to hedge the deal and avoid such a loss, arbitrageurs can turn to the financial futures market. Treasury-bond futures are traded on the Chicago Board of Trade. The contract calls for delivery of 8-percent coupon fifteen-year bonds or their equivalent. The Marathon bonds had a similar maturity (twelve years). One could have hedged the value of the Marathon bonds by selling bond futures against the position. On November 20, 1981, the March 1982 bond futures were selling at $64^{22}/_{32}$. When Marathon Oil dropped to its low price on January 27, 1982, the bond futures dropped to $59^{15}/_{32}$. Thus, a gain in the short position in bond futures would have offset the drop in the bond's value.

In addition to hedging the risks stemming from long-term interest-rate fluctuations, the arbitrageur can hedge his cost of carrying a position. Interest expense is the largest expense of running an arbitrage business. Assume again in the Marathon–U.S. Steel example that the average spread was 4 points and that an $80 position had to be financed for five months on 50-percent margin at the broker call rate. The broker call rate in November 1981 was $14^1/_2$ percent. The interest cost associated with holding Marathon Oil to the closing of the deal would be about $2.40, more than half the spread. The broker call rate at the close of the deal was $15^3/_4$ percent. If the position had been financed at that rate, the interest cost would have been $2.62, resulting in a substantial reduction in net profit per share ($1.38 rather than $1.60).

To hedge against rising finance charges, the arbitrageur can turn to the Treasury-bill futures market. Three-month T-bill futures are traded on the Chicago Mercantile Exchange in denominations of $1 million. In November 1981, the March 1982 contracts were quoted at 89.45 percent of face value. Each 1-percent move in the contract meant a $2,500 change in face value. The arbitrageur can sell $1 million of T-bill futures for every $1 million of bank loans obtained to finance the Marathon Oil position. Hence the arbitrageur would sell one contract against every 25,000 shares of Marathon Oil. From November 1981 through March 1982, the bill contract fell 2.06 points. This resulted in a 21-cent profit per Marathon Oil share, which almost completely offset the increased interest expense for the position.

Stock-Index Futures

The same market volatility that prompted the development of interest-rate futures in the 1970s as a means of hedging interest-rate risks has contributed to the introduction of futures contract on the Standard and Poor's 500 composite index and other market averages. Started in the spring of 1982 on the Index and Option market of the Chicago Mercantile Exchange, the S&P 500 futures contract has become the largest and fastest-growing stock-index futures contract at any exchange. These futures contracts provide investors with a means of hedging against adverse market movements. They also allow investors to take advantage of broad market moves.

Given the extreme volatility and upward movement of stock-market prices since mid-1982, the appeal of these futures is all the more pronounced. The Standard and Poor's 500 Index is made up of 400 industrial companies, 40 public utilities, 20 transportation companies, and 40 financial companies and reflects approximately 80 percent of the value of all New York Stock Exchange issues currently being traded. Unlike ordinary commodity futures, which require delivery dates and carrying charges, S&P 500 futures contracts require a cash settlement with no physical delivery of an underlying commodity or resulting payment for that commodity. Like other futures contracts, a margin deposit is required when the contract is opened. Each futures position is marked-to-market, or revalued to reflect the daily market movements at the close of each business day. Any difference between the current day's price and the price of the futures contract would be credited or debited from the holder's margin account. If the debit were substantial, one could be subject to a margin call. On the final day of trading in the futures contract, there is one last reevaluation of the contract against the price of the S&P Index and the difference is either paid or collected by the holder. An S&P 500 futures position generally would be held until expiration (if trends seem favorable) or could be closed prior to expiration with an offsetting transaction.

The value of each futures contract equals the futures price times $500. The minimum trading increment is 5 percent of the $500, or $25. So if the investor was long a March futures contract that settled at 150.88, the contract had been held to settlement date, and the S&P 500 closing price for that day was 152.96. His profit would be the difference between the S&P closing price and the contract's price multiplied by 500.

$$152.96 - 150.88 = 2.08$$
$$2.08 \times 500 = \$1,040$$

Thus the profit for the contract holder would be $1,040.

Index Options

Futures contracts provide significant leverage for the investor since only a small commitment of capital is needed to participate in transactions with substantial dollar values. But there is a risk that the initial margin deposit will be offset by market losses, requiring additional margin deposits. This risk can be reduced with an option on the contract. S&P 500 futures options provide limited risk in the same manner that options on listed stocks do—the full amount that can be lost is the premium paid for the option. There are no additional margin calls since the premium paid represents the holder's total financial obligation. A call option gives the holder the right to purchase the underlying futures contract while a put enables the holder to sell the underlying futures. S&P 500 futures options trade on the same time cycle as their underlying futures contracts. These options provide investors with a clearly defined and limited level of risk with which to participate in the possible gains or protection to be had against market movements through futures contracts in the S&P 500 Index.

While the Chicago Mercantile Exchange's S&P 500 is the largest futures contract of its type, it is not the only one. There is a contract on the New York Futures Exchange that represents about 500 of the 1,500 stocks on the New York Stock Exchange (NYSE). It, too, trades at values equivalent to 500 times the index, with each full point worth $500 but with $1/_{100}$-point price increments worth $5 each. The Kansas City Board of Trade has a contract based on Value Line's 1700 stock index. These differing centers of index futures, as well as the related options contracts, provide arbitrageurs with a variety in market selection for similar entities. Thus, arbitrage opportunities often exist in intermarket transactions.

Stock-Index-Futures Arbitrage

The true arbitrage action in futures markets is to buy the cash commodity and sell a futures contract, thereby locking in a spread. Since stock-index futures settle in cash, not a portfolio of stocks, the underlying commodity cannot be delivered and a classic futures arbitrage is not possible. Suppose one were to buy a portfolio of stocks that perfectly tracked the movement of the index and to sell a stock index futures contract against the portfolio. To close out the position on the last trading day of the futures contract, all stocks in the portfolio would have to be sold at their closing prices. The arbitrageur tries to develop a proxy of as few as twenty stocks that will closely track the original index. The risk is that the proxy and index will fall out of line.

But other arbitrage opportunities do arise. Differences between the options on futures and the futures themselves create arbitrage possibilities.

A recently popular form of arbitrage is intermarket arbitrage. It arises because most major indexes are correlated. To effect such transactions, the ratios of contracts bought to contracts sold must be carefully analyzed. For instance, the closing values of the S&P 500 composite and the June 1983 futures contract on March 18, 1983, were 151.25 and 152.25 respectively. The NYSE composite and the June 1983 futures closed at 87.40 and 87.75. The S&P futures closed at a 0.7-percent premium while the NY futures closed at 0.4 percent premium. The ratio of values of the S&P to the NYSE index is 151.25:87.40, or 1.73. The strategy is to buy seven low-premium contracts (NYSE) and sell four high-premium contracts (S&P). (Note that 7:4 = 1.75.)

The contracts closed at 153.80 (S&P) and 88.85 (NYSE) the following day. The profit on the transaction would be:

$$7 \times (88.85 - 87.75) - 4 \times (153.80 - 152.25) = 150 \text{ points,}$$
or $750 before costs

Stock-Index Options

In addition to futures contracts and options futures contracts on the major stock indexes, straight index options that do not involve futures contracts are now available. These cash-settlement options are traded in a similar manner to ordinary stock options except when exercised: the option writer pays the holder the difference between the striking price of the option and the close of the option's underlying index times a multiplier. These multipliers are fixed by the exchange where the option is traded and determine the total dollar value of each point difference between the option and the underlying index. For example, a holder of a September 145 call on the XYZ Index exercises his option when the Index closes at 150. Assuming a given multiplier of 100, the writer would have to pay the holder the difference times the multiplier (in this case, $5 × 100, or $500).

The Chicago Board Options Exchange is the leading trader of index options. Its CBOE 100 option, based on the S&P 500, became the most popular device. Less than one year old, the CBOE 100 option, whose name was soon changed to S&P 500, was the first contract on an index where a commodity futures registration was not required for the broker-dealer; it quickly became the top-selling contract. Index options are also traded and/or approved for trading on the American Stock Exchange (AMEX) and the New York Stock Exchange. The AMEX started two options, one based on twenty stocks that closely match the Dow Jones Industrial Index and the second called the AMEX Market Value Index. New options contracts continue to be developed.

Intermarket opportunities for locking in the spread have grown as a result of these vehicles. For example, the success of the S&P option has prompted the Chicago Mercantile Exchange to develop an identical futures contract for the same stocks and with the same expiration months as the option, thus providing the opportunity for conversions and reverse conversion between the two. As a hedging device, one could use a private portfolio made up of the AMEX twenty stock index and effect conversions with the identical options.

Summary

There are other important forms of risk arbitrage besides merger arbitrage. Convertible securities, spin-offs, and stubs have long provided opportunities for the risk arbitrageur. In principle, these situations are similar to basic merger arbitrage, especially in the analysis of both the return on investment and the value of the securities.

There are also new instruments that have given the risk arbitrageur other tools to ply his trade. Stock options and interest-rate futures are now important vehicles for hedging transactions in merger arbitrage and other forms of risk arbitrage. They also provide exciting arbitrage opportunities in themselves.

9
MERGER AND
ACQUISITION LAW

There is a wide body of law that affects the procedures as well as the successful consummation of a merger or tender offer deal. Previous chapters have outlined how such issues as prenotification filings, antitrust matters, public disclosure requirements, and state takeover statutes are important in the arbitrageur's analysis of a particular deal, and how the potential for any violations can either substantially delay its consummation or kill it entirely.

This chapter provides a basic overview of the current laws and relevant statutes which apply to tender offer and merger activity.

Hart-Scott-Rodino Notification Rules

Title II of the Hart-Scott-Rodino Antitrust Improvements Act of 1976 (included in Section 7A of the Clayton Act), became effective on September 5, 1978. This act prevents the consummation of a merger or substantial corporate acquisition until the Federal Trade Commission and the Justice Department have had the opportunity to review the proposed transaction in light of federal antitrust laws, particularly Section 7 of the Clayton Act. After the filing of the proper forms, the law requires a premerger notification ("file-and-wait") period of fifteen calendar days in the case of a cash tender offer or thirty calendar days for all other types of transactions. Section 7A essentially provides government agencies with the time to consider possible antitrust violations. But the file-and-wait requirements apply only to a deal's legal consummation, closing, and transfer of title. Other steps in the transaction may be taken.

History and Background

As both the Justice Department and the Federal Trade Commission attempted to block illegal mergers and acquisitions under the antitrust provisions of the Clayton Act in the 1970s, it became apparent that their authority to uphold the law was seriously hampered by a lack of proper information.

Prior to the Hart-Scott-Rodino Act, there was no requirement that the antitrust agencies be advised of proposed mergers and acquisitions, nor was there any requirement that the agencies be provided with information in a report form or that the transaction be subject to waiting periods before consummation. The Hart-Scott-Rodino Act allows government agencies to conduct more thorough investigations and to present the required facts before a federal judge in time to block a suspect merger before its consummation.

The Waiting Period

As noted earlier, both the acquirer and the target corporation are required to file. However, in the case of various types of acquisitions, including open-market purchases and tender offers, the acquirer bears responsibility since the initial waiting period is triggered by the acquiring company's filing. The target of a hostile acquisition cannot delay the file-and-wait period through noncompliance or by filing at the last possible moment (fifteen calendar days after the bidder files its form, generally ten calendar days in a cash tender). This protective clause does not apply to other kinds of acquisitions. In those, the initial waiting period does not commence until both parties have filed. In addition, no matter which of the two antitrust agencies investigates the transaction (only one clearance is given), both can request further information from the companies during the initial file-and-wait period. Any request made for additional data during the initial waiting period extends that period (ten calendar days for a cash tender offer, twenty calendar days for other acquisitions) after the date the material is received by the requesting agency. Again, failure of a target's compliance in a tender does not delay the waiting period. Further, the waiting periods under the Hart-Scott-Rodino Act do not include the day filing actually is made; the waiting periods begin on the day after the filing.

Providing that certain conditions are satisfied—most importantly, that neither agency intends to take any enforcement action—the agencies may terminate a waiting period before its conclusion. In the past, companies were required to establish that early termination was necessary from a business standpoint (e.g., that a firm's existing financial and contractual obligations and relationships would be adversely affected unless early termination was granted). This is no longer required. Early termination is of particular importance during hostile or competing tender offers, where prenotification requirements may otherwise favor a particular party. However, since the guidelines emphasize that the filing requirements should have a neutral effect, the agencies generally will not approve early termination to assist a competing suitor. Tender-offer waiting periods can be amended or extended if the bidder increases the number of shares sought over its initial notification threshold, or if the terms of the offer are changed from cash to noncash (or vice versa). In the case of two-step acquisitions, both transactions usually are treated together and forms for both steps generally are filed simultaneously.

Exemptions

Several types of acquisitions are exempted from filing:

1. The acquisition of options and warrants is exempt because they are not technically voting securities and the rules apply only to the acquisition of assets or voting securities. The acquisition of convertible voting securities also is exempt. However, their conversion may require a filing.

2. An acquisition by an acquiring company already holding 50 percent of a target's voting securities is exempt and does not require a filing. This is especially important to second-step merger deals.

3. So-called intraperson transactions (where the acquirer and target are the same entity) are exempt. This includes a corporation's repurchase of its own voting securities. It does not apply, however, to the formation of new corporations which will not be wholly owned, an important consideration in leveraged buy-outs.

4. Securities acquired solely "for the purpose of investment" are exempt, provided that they do not result in the purchaser's holding in excess of 10 percent of the issuer's outstanding voting stock and the holder has no intention of participating in the firm's business activities or decisions. If the investor is a so-called institutional investor and certain other conditions are met, an acquisition for the "purpose of investment" is exempt so long as it does not result in the purchaser's holding more than 10 percent or $15 million of the acquired company's stock, whichever is greater.

No separate exemption is allowed to arbitrageurs, who must qualify under the institutional-investor exemption regulation. This usually should pose no problem, since few arbitrageurs are likely to exceed the 10-percent limit of a target's outstanding voting stock and may be considered, for purposes of this exemption, as broker-dealers, one of the institutional investors itemized in the regulations.

Who Must File

There are three main criteria for a reportable acquisition: commerce, size of person, and size of acquisition. All three criteria must be satisfied before a filing is required.

1. The commerce test requires either the acquirer or the target to be engaged in some form of actual commerce or activity affecting commerce as defined in the Clayton Act or by Federal Trade Commission regulations.

2. The size-of-person test requires that either the acquirer or target have total assets or total net sales of at least $100 million. Generally, if one party fulfills the $100-million requirement, the other need only have $10 million in total assets or net sales. Assets are determined by the entity's most recent balance sheet (no older than fifteen months); net sales by its most recent income statement. This figure generally does not include any funds borrowed for the purpose of a takeover. Thus, an artificially inflated balance sheet resulting from short-term acquisition borrowing generally will not meet the size-of-person test.

The acquiring company is defined as all entities controlled, directly or indirectly, by an ultimate parent entity. Thus, the ultimate parent entity may or may not be the actual direct beneficiary of a merger or takeover deal but would retain control over the subsidiary's or affiliate's activities. A company controls another when it holds either 50 percent of an entity's voting stock or has a currently exercisable right to designate a majority of the board of directors for that entity. For purposes of the size-of-person test, an ultimate parent entity's total assets or net sales must reflect a complete consolidation of the parent's affiliates and subsidiary's assets or sales, regardless of how these amounts are generally reported.

3. The size-of-acquisition test involves two criteria: the dollar-value test and the percentage test, either of which must be satisfied:

A) Under the Hart-Scott-Rodino Act, these tests are satisfied if the acquiring company, as a result of the acquisition, would hold either 10 percent or more of the acquired company's voting securities or assets, or more than $15 million, in the aggregate, of the acquired company's voting securities and assets.

B) However, the Federal Trade Commission's regulations modify the act so that an acquisition that satisfies the 10-percent test but does not satisfy the $15-million test still will be exempt so long as I) in the case of a voting securities acquisition, the acquisition will not confer control of the acquired entity or, if it does confer control, the acquired entity (together with all companies it controls directly or indirectly) has annual net sales or total assets of less than $25 million; and II) in the case of an asset acquisition, the acquisition will not result in the acquiring company's holding more than $15 million of the acquired company's assets.

Securities held by the acquirer "as a result of" an acquisition are defined as all voting securities of the same issues that the acquiring company will hold after consummation, including those it already holds. Thus, the size-of-acquisition test is determined according to the percentage or dollar value of voting securities or assets held as a result of an acquisition. While the value of previously held securities may be added to the acquired assets (in order to reach the $15-million trigger point), previously held *assets* are *not* included in the determination of whether subsequent acquisition of voting securities meets the test.

Other Reporting Thresholds

Subsequent filings may be required if the acquiring company seeks to make additional acquisitions of voting securities or assets of the acquired company. In the case of voting-securities acquisitions, reports must be filed before the acquiring company can purchase additional voting securities that, together with its previously acquired stock, will result in holdings of 15 percent (assuming that the size-of-acquisition test was satisfied initially by crossing the $15-million threshold), 25 percent and 50 percent of the outstanding voting securities of the acquired company. In the case of an asset acquisition, the 10-percent/$15-million size-of-acquisition test continues to determine the need for further filings.

Current Acquisition Rules and Practices

The effect of Section 7A on a current acquisition practice is especially relevant given the popularity of multistep forms and lock-up devices. In typical multistep transactions where an "any and all" tender offer is followed by a merger, the 50-percent threshold is crossed during the tender-offer step, thus exempting the merger from a second waiting period. If the tender offer were for less than 50 percent, the subsequent merger could be reported separately. Therefore, the general practice is to file for both the tender offer and merger simultaneously or, failing that, as close together as possible.

Antitrust Law

As noted in Chapter 7, antitrust violations are a target's most powerful legal defense against a hostile bidder. A positive ruling on an antitrust violation can stop an offer, which is why it is called a showstopper. Intermittent litigation can significantly affect an offer's timetable. It is for this reason that arbitrageurs should be familiar with the basic federal antitrust statutes and their application to mergers and acquisitions. Because of the breadth and complexity of this area of the law, I will present only an overview of the relevant statutes.

The three main antitrust statutes are the Sherman Antitrust Act, the Federal Trade Commission Act, and the Clayton Antitrust Act.

The Sherman Antitrust Act

Passed in 1890, the Sherman Act represented an early attempt on the part of the U.S. government to end the abuses of corporate power by the giant trusts that emerged during the boom years after the Civil War. The rapid growth of such industrial monopolies as the sugar, oil, and whiskey trusts in the 1880s created an unprecedented concentration of corporate power. Such trusts abused their monopoly positions by forcing secret rebates and manipulating consumers through controlled production and price-fixing. These anticompetitive measures often were accompanied by blatant financial corruption and scandal—bribery, market manipulation, and fraud. Farmers and laborers were particularly exploited. The social and economic dislocation that resulted created a strong political reform movement whose aim was directed chiefly at the large trusts and monopolies considered most responsible for such abuses. In response, Congress created the Interstate Commerce Commission in 1887 to regulate the railroads and passed the Sherman Act three years later to encourage healthy competition and eliminate corporate conspiracies.

Although the Sherman Act contains seven sections, the first two are most important for the arbitrageur.

Section 1 makes "every contract, combination in the form

of trust or otherwise, or conspiracy, in restraint of trade or commerce among the several States, or with foreign nations" illegal.

Section 2 forbids "every person who shall monopolize, or attempt to monopolize, or combine or conspire with any other person or persons, to monopolize any part of the trade or commerce among the several States, or with foreign nations."

The act makes violations of these statutes crimes punishable by fines and/or imprisonment, with treble damages awarded to those victimized by violators.

The language of the law is deliberately general and provides no precise definition of what is meant by "restraint of trade" or "attempt to monopolize." Instead, the act relies on the interpretation of existing common law practices. The blanket prohibitions of the Sherman Act frequently were applied in its first years to all business combinations, regardless of their utility or reasonableness. This practice ended with the Standard Oil case of 1911, in which the Supreme Court declared that the act prohibited only "unreasonable" conduct. It thereby created the "rule of reason" as a test against most agreements thought to be in violation of the act. The rule-of-reason interpretation does not apply to practices which are such obvious restraints of trade that their mere existence creates a violation. These "per se" antitrust violations include price-fixing, group boycotts, concerted refusals to deal, market-allocation agreements, and the like. Per se violations need only be shown to have occurred, while a litigant alleging another antitrust violation must prove not only its existence but also that it was unreasonable.

Federal Trade Commission Act

The limitations on the Sherman Act under the 1911 decision gave impetus for passage of further antitrust laws. Accordingly, in 1914, Congress passed the Federal Trade

Commission Act and the Clayton Act. The Federal Trade Commission Act set up a commission with the powers to investigate unfair trade practices, provide improved enforcement procedures, and create guidelines as to which trade practices were considered lawful and which were prohibited.

The Federal Trade Commission Act was designed to prevent "unfair methods of competition in or affecting commerce, and unfair or deceptive acts or practices in or affecting commerce." The commission was given wide latitude to determine exactly what constituted unfair methods of competition on a case-by-case basis. The commission also is responsible for the enforcement of the FTC Act, the Clayton Act (along with the Justice Department), and several consumer-protection statutes.

The Clayton Antitrust Act

One of Congress's major intents in passing the Clayton Act in 1914 was to define as unlawful certain practices not specifically identified in the Sherman Act.

The Clayton Act, along with the Robinson-Patman Act amendments, prohibits certain mergers, price discrimination, and exclusive dealing arrangements. Section 7 of the Clayton Act prohibits any corporate merger "where the effect . . . may be to substantially lessen competition" or that may "tend to create a monopoly." Passed in 1936, the Robinson-Patman Act amended Section 2 of the Clayton Act, broadly rewriting the price-discrimination provisions of the act. This amendment, together with the Cellar-Kefauver Act of 1950, represent the two major amendments to the original Clayton Act. The Cellar-Kefauver Act is of particular relevance since it expanded the scope of Section 7 in a number of ways, including bringing asset acquisitions within its scope.

As noted in Chapter 7, the most common grounds for antitrust violations under the Clayton Act involve horizontal mergers, where there would be a lessening of competition by direct competitors combining to do business in the same general product or service and in the same geographic area. A recent application of this prohibition was in the Mobil Oil–Marathon takeover battle. Mobil's bid for Marathon was permanently halted on antitrust grounds on December 1, 1981, little more than a month after its initial $5.1-billion offer was announced.

Other grounds for antitrust violations under Section 7 of the Clayton Act include the merger of one of only a few potential competitors and a company already competing in a highly concentrated market, if the merger is likely to result in a substantial lessening of competition.

Justice Department Merger Guidelines

New, more lenient guidelines issued by the Justice Department on June 14, 1984, explain the standards used by the department to oppose an acquisition on antitrust grounds under Section 7 of the Clayton Act. The effect of the revised guidelines has been to clarify previous enforcement standards and to narrow their focus. The intent of the guidelines is to prevent the accumulation of undue "market power" resulting from a merger and to permit those mergers that are deemed to have either a beneficial or neutral effect upon the marketplace. Market power is determined through analysis of market concentration and market shares of the companies competing in the market. The guidelines use an index, called the Hirschman-Herfindahl Index, to measure market power. This index, created in 1982, is derived by adding the sum of the square of the market share of each producer in the market under question.

To determine whether the Justice Department will challenge a merger or acquisition, the increase in the Hirschman-Herfindahl Index due to the merger (determined by multiplying the market shares of the merging parties and then multiplying that result by two) must be compared to the overall postmerger Hirschman-Herfindahl Index. Depending upon which of three classifications the Hirschman-Herfindahl Index falls within (0–999, unconcentrated; 1000–1800, moderately concentrated; more than 1800, highly concentrated), an increase in the index will result in a particular Justice Department response. The higher the overall postmerger Hirschman-Herfindahl Index, the lower an increase must be to prompt Justice Department action. For instance, any merger that creates a total postmerger Hirschman-Herfindahl Index of 999 or less is considered to be safe from antitrust challenge by the Justice Department, regardless of the merger's increase in the Hirschman-Herfindahl Index. However, it is "more likely than not" that the department will challenge a merger that increases the Hirschman-Herfindahl Index more than 100 points in a moderately concentrated market. In a highly concentrated market, the same result can be expected for an increase of between 50 and 100 points. See the chart on the facing page.

The Federal Trade Commission also has issued its own enforcement policy statement. This statement, which is expressly limited to horizontal transactions, does not set forth any specific quantitative standards. Rather, it indicates in general terms the type of analysis that will be used and emphasizes that the revised Justice guidelines will be afforded considerable weight by the Federal Trade Commission. The only points on which the two take different positions appear to be the commission's somewhat more relaxed view toward defense arguments of enhanced efficiency and the "failing company" defense.

Whether the Justice Department or the Federal Trade Commission assumes the review of a particular merger is decided on a case-by-case basis. Traditionally, the Justice Department concentrates on mergers involving the structure of basic industries, such as steel and aluminum, while the Federal Trade Commission generally concentrates on

The Hirschman-Herfindahl Index

The index is calculated by squaring the percentage market share of each firm in the market and then adding those squares.* The result of this calculation will provide a concentration index for the market that will, in large part, determine the Justice Department's approach to the merger. In addition, the Justice Department will use the Hirschman-Herfindahl Index to measure the increase in concentration resulting from the merger. This figure is calculated by doubling the product of the percentage shares of the two merging firms.†

The Justice Department's guidelines set forth the following thresholds:

Hirschman-Herfindahl Index	Increase in Concentration	Justice Department Challenge
0–999	Not applicable	Extremely unlikely
1000–1800	Less than 100‡ More than 100	Unlikely More likely than not
Above 1800§	Less than 50 50–100 More than 100	Unlikely More likely than not// Likely

* If there are four firms in a market with shares of 30%, 30%, 20%, and 20% respectively, the Hirschman-Herfindahl Index would be 2600 ($30^2 + 30^2 + 20^2 + 20^2$).

† If Companies A and B, each with 8% of a market, merge, the increase in concentration would be 2AB, or $2 \times 8 \times 8 = 128$. This is the result of the simple algebraic equation: $(A+B)^2 = A^2 + 2AB + B^2$.

‡ Concentration increases of almost 100 points would be attributable to mergers of the following size: 25%/2%, 16%/3%, 12%/4%, 10%/5%, 8%/6%, 7%/7%.

§ In many cases, the shares of the smaller firms in a market may not be known. However, since the Hirschman-Herfindahl Index deals in squares of market percentages, smaller shares have an increasingly *de minimis* impact on the Hirschman-Herfindahl Index. Mathematically, it can be shown that the total Hirschman-Herfindahl Index attributable to the smaller unknown firms cannot exceed the product of the smallest known market share and the total unknown market share. Thus, if the four largest firms in a market have a combined 75% share and are known to have shares of 30%, 25%, 15%, and 5%, the remaining firms can account for no more than 125 (25×5) Hirschman-Herfindahl Index points.

// In contrast, under the now-outdated 1968 guidelines, the Justice Department was likely to challenge a merger in a less highly concentrated market (below 1800) if an increase from 50–90 were to occur. In a highly concentrated market (above 1800) the 1968 guidelines would have authorized a challenge if an increase of 30–40 occurred. While the Hirschman-Herfindahl Index was not implemented until 1982, the Justice Department had less formal market concentration tests before then.

more consumer-oriented industries, such as food products and health care. There is no definitive guideline, however, and cases are assumed by an agency for historical reasons or because one of the agencies has more experience and specialization in a particular area. For example, the Federal Trade Commission, not the Justice Department, generally investigates mergers involving oil companies while Justice shares responsibility with the commission for insurance industry mergers.

Summary

The one obstacle that can terminate a prospective merger is the objection of one of the two antitrust authorities, the Justice Department and the Federal Trade Commission. Therefore, the arbitrageur must pay constant attention to changes in the antitrust law made by the courts and through legislation. He also must be sensitive to changes in philosophy and attitude among the antitrust authorities, including elected and appointed officials, and especially by the President. The Hart-Scott-Rodino Act, passed in the late 1970s, establishes a procedure to bring every proposed merger before the authorities. The two basic acts that concern antitrust decisions remain the Clayton and Sherman acts. The Justice Department now issues guidelines that are very useful in determining the likelihood of government objections to mergers.

10
TAXES AND
MERGER ARBITRAGE

The main tax issue in arbitrage is determining whether the transaction is taxable to the shareholders. In the most general sense, an exchange of securities is tax-free and typically falls into one of seven reorganization categories. A cash transaction is typically taxable to the shareholders.

How an arbitrage profit is taxed can significantly affect the return on the investment. We have discussed this at some length in Chapter 3. But tax issues can be quite complicated. They invariably require the advice of competent accountants and attorneys. Moreover, professional arbitrageurs retain advisers who specialize in just such situations. In this chapter, we will cover some of the more technical and complex tax problems the arbitrageur will face. The reader who wishes to wend his way through the tangled tax thicket will find a highly technical guide in Appendix B.

Boot

In a tax-free exchange, the holding period of the original stock owned becomes the holding period of the new stock received in the merger. Similarly, the cost basis of the old stock is the cost basis of the new stock. Currently, the long-term holding period is six months and a day.

When consideration other than the stock or securities is given in a tax-free reorganization, that consideration is known as boot. But computing the tax due on the boot can be a very complex affair. In general, if a shareholder receives boot as well as qualifying stock or securities, his gain, if any, is to be recognized, but in an amount not in excess of the boot.

Let us take the most simple example of a Type A reorganization. The acquiring company is purchasing the acquired company, 50 percent for stock and the remaining 50 percent for cash. One stockholder receives all stock in the transaction and enjoys the advantage of a completely tax-free exchange. The new tax basis of the stock is received the same as the tax basis of the old stock, and its holding period includes the period during which the old stock was held. But another stockholder receives all cash. The profit on the transaction is taxable as capital gain (assuming the stock is a capital asset in his hands), long- or short-term, depending on the holding period. It is as if he had sold the stock.

In the real world, however, it is unlikely that one investor will get all the cash and the other all stock. Typically, each will get a portion of his total consideration in both cash and stock. In such cases, the consideration in the form other than the qualifying stock is subject to taxes. (If the new consideration results in a loss to the shareholder, that loss is not deductible for tax purposes.)

In circumstances where a gain is realized, one determines the tax liability by assessing the portion of the consideration that is boot against the realized gain. The following example makes this clear.

Cost of stock: $100
Total consideration received in merger: $150

1. $75 worth of stock
2. $75 in cash = boot
Realized gain = $50

In this example, boot exceeds the realized gain, so the full realized gain will be recognized for tax purposes. Let's look at a slightly different situation:

Cost of stock: $75
Total consideration received in merger: $150
1. $100 worth of stock
2. $50 in cash = boot
Realized gain = $75

In this case, we would recognize only $50 of the realized gain for tax purposes because the boot came to only $50.

But how is the gain taxed once it is recognized? The answer unfortunately is not simple. The law states that if the exchange has "the effect of the distribution of a *dividend*," the gain will be treated as dividend income to each distributor to the extent of his ratable share of the undistributed accumulated earnings of the acquired company. The remainder, if any, of the gain recognized is treated as gain from the exchange of property (i.e., capital gain unless the shareholder is a dealer in securities and the shares are not properly identified and held for investment). A full analysis of the phrase "has the effect of the distribution of a *dividend*" would be too complicated for this book. In general, the same principles used in determining whether a stock redemption is to be treated as a sale or exchange or a dividend are applied in determining the character of the gain. However, an essential point is that if a shareholder's proportionate share of the undistributed accumulated earnings was $50 or more, $50 would be the maximum amount of dividend income that could result from the exchange. If the ratable share of undistributed accumulated earnings came to, say, $25, the maximum amount of dividend income would be $25. If all or some portion of the distribution resulted in capital gain for tax purposes, short- or long-term treatment would depend on the length of time that the stock was held.

Substantial Disproportionate Redemption

Again, let's stay in the real world for a moment. Assume that a typical two-step merger is undertaken. In the first step, a cash tender offer is made for 49 percent of the company. In the second step, stock is exchanged to complete the merger. The two steps taken together can qualify as a Type A reorganization (assuming the "continuity of interest" test is satisfied). A shareholder may get all cash, all stock, or a combination in the transaction. If the shareholder receives all cash, it is taxed as a capital gain. If he receives all stock, it is tax-free. A combination of stock and cash will result in some tax liability on the cash part, the boot.

There is a test that, if met, results in the recognized portion of the gain to be taxed as a capital gain. If the shareholder receives proportionately less stock in the new corporation than he had in the acquired corporation, he may be deemed to have a substantially disproportionate redemption. In order for the redemption to qualify as substantially disproportionate, immediately after the redemption the shareholder must own less than 80 percent of the percentage of outstanding voting stock and less than 80 percent of the percentage of common stock (whether or not voting) he held immediately before the redemption. If the redemption is substantially disproportionate for a shareholder, the gain is recognized as an exchange, and not as a dividend.

Recent tender laws have reduced occasions where stockholders get disproportionate allocations of stock and cash. But the circumstances do still arise. If the shareholder is a corporation, it may prefer dividend income and may try to arrange to equal or exceed the 80-percent redemption level. The noncorporate shareholder will usually prefer capital gains. It is another aspect of the arbitrageur's job to anticipate such possibilities.

Liquidations

When a corporation liquidates completely, the gain on the distributions is considered a capital gain for tax purposes. The gain is equal to the amount of the proceeds less the cost of the shares. The holding period of the original shares determines whether the gain is short- or long-term. But there are a variety of complications and we will address several of the most important ones.

Ideally, a corporation will be able to sell all of its assets and distribute the cash to shareholders. In reality, there are often times when assets are not easily divisible. A company may distribute shares it owns on a proportionate basis, for example. This is straightforward. But a corporation may also have assets that cannot be divided easily or sold separately for cash. In order to liquidate, the company may place those assets in a noncorporate entity (a "liquidating trust"); the shareholder would then receive an interest in this new entity. How is the new entity valued? The arbitrageur must make some assumptions that may not square with the Internal Revenue Service's ultimate determination. The ongoing tax status of the entity must be assessed. There is no escape from the need of good tax counsel in these circumstances. But the arbitrageur must understand the issues in order to know when to call in specialized counsel.

Section 337

The arbitrageur will also want to be certain about the tax status of the liquidated assets. A corporation could be subjected to a form of double taxation if it does not abide by certain requirements. When assets are sold, for example, they may be subject to taxes. When they are then distributed to shareholders, the shareholders are again subject to taxes. The Internal Revenue Service has established a procedure where corporations are exempt from taxes. It falls under Section 337 of the Internal Revenue Code. That section allows a corporation to not realize a gain on sale of assets if the sale is completed within a year (except for certain inventory and other items such as recapture of depreciation and investment credit). There are technical problems that sometimes disqualify a corporation from Section 337. To the arbitrageur, it is of utmost importance to know whether the liquidation falls under this section.

Holding Period

If a complete liquidation takes place over time, and most do, how does one determine the holding period for tax purposes? Again, to qualify for long-term tax rates, the investment must be held for six months and a day. Let's say that a company's intention to liquidate under Section 337 is announced on July 1 and the arbitrageur buys stock that day. As a Section 337 liquidation, all assets of the company must be distributed within a year after the plan is adopted. The arbitrageur buys the stock for $100 and the first distribution is $50. This is considered a recovery of cost. The new tax basis of the holding is now $50. On December 30, the company distributes $75. The $25 gain is considered short-term. If the corporation instead had sold all its assets and issued a $50 distribution in December, the arbitrageur's tax basis would be zero. The remaining $25, if distributed in January or afterward, would be a long-term gain. It is of course especially advantageous to have a cooperative corporation in the matter of the timing of distributions. From time to time, the question of constructive receipt is raised by the Internal

Revenue Service. Constructive receipt means that the shareholder is liable for the taxes when the gain could have been received, as opposed to when it actually was received.

Partial Liquidations

Partial-liquidation treatment applies only to noncorporate shareholders. A partial liquidation involves a corporate contraction or a termination of one of two or more active businesses engaged in by the distributing corporation. The corporation sells a part of its assets and determines the proportion of assets that it comes to. This determination, it is important to realize, is made on a fair-market-value basis. The shareholder takes as his cost basis the same proportion of his total payment for the shares. The gain is then treated as long- or short-term capital gains, depending on the holding period. Note that this differs from a periodic distribution during a complete liquidation, where the distribution is considered a return of capital rather than taken as a capital gain.

Stretched-out Liquidations

Liquidations that take more than one year are subject to similar tax treatment as the Section 337 complete liquidation for the shareholder. Distributions are considered recovery of cost until a zero tax basis is reached. They then are taxed—as short- or long-term capital gains—according to the length of the holding period.

Self-Tenders

When there is a tender for stock in a situation that does not involve a merger, the taxability of the boot must be determined. And again, basically the same requirements are involved. The arbitrageur must assess whether he will fall under the substantially disproportionate test or the "not essentially equivalent to a dividend" test. If so, the recognized gain is capital gain (subject to "dealer" limitations). If not, the gains are considered dividends. Some arbitrageurs, as discussed, may prefer dividend income. Again, the arbitrageur must try to assess the number of shares that will be tendered and the number of shares to be accepted. If his percentage holdings in voting stock and in common stock fall below 80 percent of his percentage interest in such stock before the tender, a substantially disproportionate redemption is deemed to have occurred. Conversely, if his percentage interest in the company is not reduced as a result of the tender, the redemption will not be treated as "not essentially equivalent to a dividend." As discussed previously, the same general procedure takes place in a two-step Type A reorganization where a partial tender is made.

Summary

The taxability of gains earned on a merger-arbitrage investment will affect the rate of return as much or more than any other single factor. Unfortunately, taxability is seldom easy to determine. Generally, when a company is acquired for securities, the exchange is tax-free to the shareholders. When it is acquired for cash, it is taxable. But what happens in a merger that is paid for in both cash and stock? How is a liquidation taxed? A partial liquidation? The answers are seldom easy to determine, but they are critical in the careful determination of potential rate of return. Competent tax counsel should be consulted.

11
THE MERGER-ARBITRAGE
CHECKLIST

The practice of merger arbitrage requires constant attention and vigilance. By now, the reader should understand fully the complexity of the tasks involved, as well as the skills necessary to practice arbitrage well. If this book has given the impression that any kind of risk arbitrage is easy, I have failed. But risk arbitrage is neither esoteric nor conceptually beyond the scope of the diligent student of investments. The following checklist summarizes the key elements of merger-arbitrage. It is composed of the eleven questions an arbitrageur must be able to answer before an investment is made.

1. What is the workout value of the offer?
This is always the first step in the arbitrage process. A cash tender offer is easy to analyze. But an offering of securities may be more difficult. The arbitrageur cannot proceed until he knows the exact value of the offer being made, and how it may fluctuate under varying conditions.

2. What is the rate of return on the investment?
Once the arbitrageur knows the workout value, he must compute the actual return on the money he puts up. This will depend on his ability to borrow, interest costs, and

margin restrictions. But most important, it will depend on when the merger will be consummated and when he will receive his money.

3. How will tax considerations affect the rate of return?

Most acquisitions for cash are taxable. Most acquisitions for stock are not. But tax issues can be very complex. They will always significantly affect the potential return on the arbitrage investment. Tax counsel should be consulted.

4. When will the merger be completed?

The arbitrageur must estimate when the merger will be completed. A tender offer usually will be completed within weeks. An exchange offer can take much longer. Third-party bids and court actions can delay the process. So can government rulings by regulatory or antitrust agencies. The timing of the deal will become more clear as the process gets underway. As the timing becomes more certain, the arbitrageur might increase or decrease his investment. Timing is extremely important in determining the arbitrageur's rate of return.

5. Does the merger make business sense?

The combination of the two companies should be sensible or the deal may fall through. Is there a logical fit between the two companies? Does the acquiring company have a justifiable reason for taking over the target company? The arbitrageur also must analyze whether the price of the deal makes sense. He must determine the value of the company being acquired. Too high an offering price might jeopardize a deal. Too low a price might attract other bidders.

6. Are there antitrust matters or other regulatory objections that could kill the deal?

Most acquiring companies will explore potential antitrust questions before an offer is made. But occasionally, the Federal Trade Commission or the Justice Department will object to a deal. Most arbitrageurs will seek professional advice on the likelihood of antitrust interference. There also can be other regulatory blocks. For example, the Federal Communications Commission can make the acquisition of companies with television stations difficult.

7. Will the economic environment change?

An acquisition of an oil company might be jeopardized if oil prices suddenly start to fall. This also is true of metal companies and metal prices. A sharp rise in interest rates might make acquisitions of thrift institutions less desirable. A rising dollar will reduce the value of export companies. Answering this question again requires the arbitrageur to determine the fundamental value of the company being acquired. Economic events can affect those values and the arbitrageur must be wary.

8. How opposed is the target company's management?

An aggressive management, especially of a company with cash and assets to spend, can take extreme defensive actions. So-called Pac-Man and scorched-earth defenses have worked in the past. Normally, they will work only against acquiring companies of equal or lesser size that do not have the financial muscle to fight back. The arbitrageur, then, must assess the target's willingness to fight, as well as the acquiring company's willingness and wherewithal to fight back.

9. Does the merger conform to the nature of other mergers at the time?

Compared with many other investment strategies, risk arbitrage has a short time frame and therefore fashion does matter. If the financial community generally believes oil companies are undervalued, the acquisition of an oil company will be more likely to go through. In the long run, such an acquisition may turn out to make little business sense. The fear of inflation in the 1970s inspired many commodities mergers. Financial mergers also were common after deregulation. But acquisitions that fly in the face of prevailing fashion must be carefully assessed.

10. Has the definitive agreement been signed?

Until the definitive agreement is signed, a prospective merger is always in danger of collapse. The arbitrageur must know when the agreement is likely to be signed and whether there are any reasons for delay. Once the agreement has been signed, the timetable for completion of the merger is easier to determine.

11. Are there potential ad hoc problems?

Mergers often raise unprecedented issues. The arbitrageur must be up-to-date about the companies involved. Constant attention must be paid to news articles. Access to brokers' research is encouraged. And to repeat one last time, there is no escaping the need for constant vigilance.

Appendix A:
Proxy Statements
and Workout
Value Examples

Proxy statements and other data on workout value examples cited in Chapter 2 are contained in this Appendix. These will help the reader understand where such information is actually to be found—and how it can be found—in actual merger cases. The portions of the documents that pertain to the computation of the workout values have been highlighted with gray shading.

1. Aetna Life and Casualty Company and Geosource: merger agreement and price information

2. The Coca-Cola Company and Columbia Pictures Industries: Columbia proxy materials

3. United States Steel Corporation and Marathon Oil Company: prospectus

4. Peavey Company and ConAgra: joint proxy and prospectus; price information

Aetna Life and Casualty Company and Geosource: merger agreement and price information

GEOSOURCE INC.

2700 Post Oak Boulevard, Suite 2000
Houston, Texas 77056
Telephone (713) 961-1111, Telex 774 549

June 7, 1982

Dear Stockholder:

A Special Meeting of Stockholders of Geosource Inc. is scheduled to be held in the Consort II Room, Westin Oaks Hotel, 5011 Westheimer, Houston, Texas, on Thursday, July 1, 1982, at 9:00 A.M., Houston, Texas time.

At the Special Meeting, you will be asked to vote upon adoption of the Agreement of Merger pursuant to which Geosource will be merged into a wholly owned subsidiary of Ætna Life and Casualty Company and stockholders of Geosource (other than Ætna and its subsidiaries) will receive 1.25 shares of Ætna Common Stock for each outstanding share of Geosource Common Stock. Ætna beneficially owns approximately 29% of the shares of Geosource's outstanding Common Stock and has indicated that such shares will be voted for adoption of the Agreement of Merger.

In the accompanying material, you will find a Notice of the Special Meeting and a Proxy Statement which more fully describes the proposed merger and the Agreement of Merger and contains other information about Geosource and Ætna. In view of the significance of the proposed merger to Geosource, you are urged to study carefully the Proxy Statement, as well as the Appendices thereto.

AFTER CAREFUL CONSIDERATION, YOUR BOARD OF DIRECTORS HAS APPROVED THE PROPOSED MERGER AND RECOMMENDS THAT YOU VOTE <u>FOR</u> ADOPTION OF THE AGREEMENT OF MERGER.

Adoption of the Agreement of Merger by Geosource stockholders requires the affirmative vote of the holders of a majority of the outstanding shares of Geosource Common Stock entitled to vote thereon. It is, therefore, important that your shares be represented and voted at the Special Meeting.

Sincerely,

JOHN D. PLATT
Chairman of the Board and
Chief Executive Officer

The Coca-Cola Company and Columbia Pictures Industries: Columbia proxy materials

Columbia Pictures Industries, Inc.

711 FIFTH AVENUE

NEW YORK, NEW YORK 10022

NOTICE OF SPECIAL MEETING OF STOCKHOLDERS
To Be Held on April 30, 1982

To the Holders of Common Stock of
COLUMBIA PICTURES INDUSTRIES, INC.

NOTICE IS HEREBY GIVEN that a Special Meeting of Stockholders of COLUMBIA PICTURES INDUSTRIES, INC., a Delaware corporation ("Columbia"), will be held at Columbia's offices at 711 Fifth Avenue, 11th floor, New York, New York, on Friday, April 30, 1982 at 10:00 A.M., New York City time, for the following purposes:

(1) to consider and act on an Agreement of Merger pursuant to which Columbia will become a subsidiary of The Coca-Cola Company; and

(2) to consider and act on any other matters which may properly come before the meeting or any adjournment thereof.

The Board of Directors has fixed the close of business on April 1, 1982 as the record date for the determination of stockholders entitled to notice of, and to vote at, the meeting or any adjournment thereof. YOUR ATTENTION IS DIRECTED TO THE PROXY STATEMENT ATTACHED TO THIS NOTICE.

For the ten days immediately preceding the meeting, a list of stockholders entitled to vote at the meeting will be available for inspection during normal business hours at Columbia's offices, 711 Fifth Avenue, New York, New York 10022, for any purpose germane to the meeting.

Whether or not you expect to be present at the meeting, you are requested to sign, date and promptly return the enclosed form of proxy, which is solicited by and on behalf of the Board of Directors. A return envelope is enclosed for your convenience.

By Order of the Board of Directors,

ELLIS A. REGENBOGEN
Secretary

April 5, 1982

SUMMARY OF THE MERGER

The following is a summary of certain information concerning the proposed merger of Columbia Pictures Industries, Inc. into a directly and indirectly wholly-owned subsidiary of The Coca-Cola Company pursuant to an Agreement of Merger, dated as of March 18, 1982, as amended (the "Merger Agreement"). This summary is intended to provide certain facts and highlights from the information contained in this Joint Proxy Statement, is not intended to be a complete statement of all material features of the proposed merger and is qualified in its entirety by the more detailed information set forth elsewhere in this Joint Proxy Statement and the attached Annexes, all of which are important and should be reviewed carefully.

The Companies

The Coca-Cola Company. The Coca-Cola Company, a Delaware corporation, is primarily engaged in the manufacture and distribution of soft drink syrups and concentrates. See "Business of The Coca-Cola Company."

Columbia Pictures Industries, Inc. Columbia Pictures Industries, Inc., a Delaware corporation ("Columbia"), is primarily engaged in the production and worldwide distribution of theatrical motion pictures and television series and features. See "Business of Columbia."

The Meetings of Stockholders; Stockholder Approvals

The Coca-Cola Company. The Annual Meeting of Stockholders of The Coca-Cola Company will be held at The Adam's Mark Hotel, 2900 Briarpark Drive, Houston, Texas 77042, on Monday, May 3, 1982, at 9:00 A.M., Houston time. Only holders of record of common stock, without par value, of The Coca-Cola Company ("Common Stock of The Coca-Cola Company") at the close of business on March 22, 1982, will be entitled to vote at the Annual Meeting or any adjournment thereof. At such date, there were outstanding and entitled to vote 123,627,522 shares of Common Stock of The Coca-Cola Company, each share being entitled to one vote.

Approval of the Merger Agreement by the stockholders of The Coca-Cola Company will require the affirmative vote of the holders of a majority of the shares of Common Stock of The Coca-Cola Company voted thereon, provided that the total vote cast on the Merger Agreement represents at least 50% of the outstanding Common Stock of The Coca-Cola Company.

Columbia. The Special Meeting of Stockholders of Columbia will be held at Columbia's offices at 711 Fifth Avenue, 11th Floor, New York, New York 10022, on Friday, April 30, 1982, at 10:00 A.M., New York time. Only holders of record of common stock, par value $.10 per share, of Columbia (the "Columbia Common Stock") at the close of business on April 1, 1982 will be entitled to vote at the Special Meeting or any adjournment thereof. At April 1, 1982, there were outstanding and entitled to vote 8,445,218 shares of Columbia Common Stock, each share being entitled to one vote.

Adoption of the Merger Agreement by the stockholders of Columbia will require the affirmative vote of the holders of a majority of the outstanding shares of Columbia Common Stock.

For additional information relating to the Annual Meeting of The Coca-Cola Company and the Special Meeting of Columbia (collectively, the "Meetings"), see "Introduction."

Purposes of Meetings

At the Meetings, the stockholders of The Coca-Cola Company will be asked to approve and the stockholders of Columbia will be asked to adopt the Merger Agreement, providing for the merger of Columbia into a directly and indirectly wholly-owned subsidiary of The Coca-Cola Company (the "Merger"). Upon the effectiveness of the Merger (the "Effective Time"), each share of Columbia Common Stock issued and outstanding at the Effective Time, other than shares owned by The Coca-Cola Company or any of its subsidiaries and shares as to which appraisal rights are duly demanded (see "The

Proposed Merger—Appraisal Rights for Dissenting Stockholders"), will be converted into cash or Common Stock of The Coca-Cola Company. Each share of Columbia Common Stock that is converted into cash will be converted into the right to receive $32.625 plus an additional cash amount equal to the product of 1.2 and the average of the daily closing prices (the "Average Market Price") of Common Stock of The Coca-Cola Company on the New York Stock Exchange ("NYSE") for the 15 NYSE trading days on which Common Stock of The Coca-Cola Company was traded immediately preceding the Effective Time, as reported in the consolidated transaction reporting system (the sum of such amount and $32.625 being referred to as the "Cash Amount"). Each share of Columbia Common Stock that is converted into Common Stock of The Coca-Cola Company will be converted into 1.2 shares of Common Stock of The Coca-Cola Company plus an additional number of such shares equal to the quotient obtained by dividing $32.625 by the Average Market Price (the sum of 1.2 shares plus such additional shares being referred to as the "Stock Amount"). For additional information concerning the treatment of Columbia securities in the Merger, see "The Proposed Merger—Treatment of Columbia Securities in the Merger" and "Market Prices."

Each holder of shares of Columbia Common Stock will receive either cash, shares of Common Stock of The Coca-Cola Company or, under certain circumstances with respect to stockholders making a conditional or unconditional Cash Election (as hereinafter described), a combination of cash and shares of Common Stock of The Coca-Cola Company. See "The Proposed Merger—Cash Election and Adjustment Procedure."

Assuming conversion and exercise of all outstanding convertible securities and options to acquire or purchase Columbia Common Stock and the issuance of shares under an employment agreement with a Columbia director-employee, the aggregate number of shares of Common Stock of The Coca-Cola Company issuable and the aggregate amount of cash payable in connection with the Merger and the other transactions contemplated by the Merger Agreement will be approximately 12,245,365 shares and approximately $332,921,000, respectively.

Cash Election and Adjustment Procedure

Each record holder of Columbia Common Stock will be entitled to make a Cash Election to receive, in lieu of Common Stock of The Coca-Cola Company, the Cash Amount per share for all or a portion of such holder's shares of Columbia Common Stock. The aggregate amount of cash which The Coca-Cola Company will pay for shares of Columbia Common Stock in the Merger will, however, be as near as practicable to, but not in excess of, the "Cash Total" as defined below.

The Cash Total is (i) the product of (a) $32.625 and (b) the number of shares of Columbia Common Stock outstanding at the Effective Time (including shares purchased pursuant to agreements with certain stockholders of Columbia (the "Stockholder Agreements"), but not including any other shares of Columbia Common Stock owned by The Coca-Cola Company and its subsidiaries), less the sum of (ii) the product of the Cash Amount and the number of shares of Columbia Common Stock purchased for cash pursuant to the Stockholder Agreements and (iii) the product of the Cash Amount and the number of shares of Columbia Common Stock for which appraisal rights have been duly demanded as of the last time on which Cash Elections must be submitted.

Columbia stockholders cannot be guaranteed that any share of Columbia Common Stock covered by a Cash Election will be purchased for cash in the Merger, or that any share of Columbia Common Stock with respect to which no Cash Election is submitted will be exchanged for shares of Common Stock of The Coca-Cola Company in the Merger. CONSEQUENTLY, COLUMBIA STOCKHOLDERS SHOULD VOTE IN FAVOR OF THE MERGER ONLY IF THEY ARE WILLING TO ACCEPT EITHER CASH OR SHARES OF COMMON STOCK OF THE COCA-COLA COMPANY, WITHOUT REGARD TO THEIR PREFERENCE.

Since The Coca-Cola Company is obligated to make cash payments only in an amount equal to the Cash Total, it is possible that Columbia stockholders who make Cash Elections may not receive cash for any or all of the shares of Columbia Common Stock covered by their Cash Elections. Because some holders of Common Stock may prefer for tax or other reasons to make their Cash Elections conditional upon a specified minimum percentage of the shares covered by such Cash Election being converted into cash, the Form of Cash Election (which is being sent to all Columbia stockholders together with this Joint Proxy Statement) will allow a Columbia stockholder to make a Cash Election either conditional or unconditional. Columbia stockholders who make unconditional Cash Elections may receive cash for only a portion of the shares covered by their Cash Elections, the exact size of such cash portion being subject to variation depending on the extent to which the number of shares of Columbia Common Stock as to which Cash Elections are made exceeds that permitted by the Cash Total and the number and type of Cash Elections made by other Columbia stockholders.

If Cash Elections are made for a number of shares of Columbia Common Stock greater than that permitted by the Cash Total, shares covered by Cash Elections will be converted into Common Stock of The Coca-Cola Company or cash as follows: (1) A Cash Proration Factor will be determined by dividing the total number of shares of Columbia Common Stock with respect to which Cash Elections are made into the number of shares to be converted into cash by application of the Cash Total. (2) The number of shares of Columbia Common Stock covered by each unconditional Cash Election and by each conditional Cash Election (other than a conditional Cash Election with respect to which a record holder of Columbia Common Stock shall have specified a minimum percentage that is greater than the Cash Proration Factor) to be converted into cash will be determined by multiplying the Cash Proration Factor by the total number of shares covered by each such Cash Election. (3) Conditional Cash Elections with respect to which record holders of Columbia Common Stock shall have specified minimum percentages that are greater than the Cash Proration Factor will be selected for elimination by lot or other equitable means so as to reduce the aggregate number of shares to be converted into cash to a number as close as practicable to, but not greater than, the number of shares to be converted into cash by application of the Cash Total. Each of the shares of Columbia Common Stock covered by each conditional Cash Election so selected for elimination will be converted into the Stock Amount. The number of shares covered by the remaining conditional Cash Elections to be converted into cash will be determined by multiplying the minimum percentage specified in each such conditional Cash Election by the total number of shares covered by such conditional Cash Election. Any share of Columbia Common Stock as to which a Cash Election (either conditional or unconditional) has been made, but which, because of the Cash Total, will not be converted into cash by reason of the application of the procedure described above, will be converted into the Stock Amount.

If Cash Elections are made for a number of shares of Columbia Common Stock equal to or less than that permitted by the Cash Total, cash payments will be made for all such shares. If, however, the aggregate amount of cash paid for shares of Columbia Common Stock covered by Cash Elections is less than the Cash Total, cash payments will be made to Columbia stockholders not making Cash Elections selected by lot or other equitable means so as to result in the payment to Columbia stockholders of an aggregate amount in cash which, when considered with cash paid pursuant to Cash Elections, is as near as practicable to, but not in excess of, the Cash Total. For purposes of the selection procedure described in the preceding sentence, each record holder of Columbia Common Stock will be considered a separate stockholder unless such record holder has informed Morgan Guaranty Trust Company of New York (the "Exchange Agent") otherwise in writing. Cash payments required as a result of the selection procedure described in this paragraph will not be made for part of the shares which are owned by a record holder of Columbia Common Stock as to which no Cash Election was made. Therefore, a record holder of Columbia Common Stock will receive either Common Stock of The Coca-Cola Company or cash for all of his shares of Columbia Common Stock which are not the subject of a Cash Election, but not both.

See "The Proposed Merger—Cash Election and Adjustment Procedure" for a further description of the procedures for converting all or a portion of a holder's shares of Columbia Common Stock into cash. See also "The Proposed Merger—Federal Income Tax Considerations."

Each record holder of shares of Columbia Common Stock is receiving with this Joint Proxy Statement a Form of Cash Election which will enable the stockholder to elect to receive the Cash Amount per share, subject to the Cash Total, in exchange for some or all of such record holder's shares of Columbia Common Stock. The Form of Cash Election or a facsimile thereof, accompanied by certificates for shares of Columbia Common Stock or a guaranty of delivery, must be received by the Exchange Agent no later than the Election Deadline, which is 5:00 P.M., New York time, on such date as is announced by The Coca-Cola Company, in a news release delivered to the Dow Jones News Service, as the last day on which Forms of Cash Election will be accepted. Such date will be no earlier than the date of the Special Meeting of Stockholders of Columbia and will be at least five business days and no more than 20 business days following the news release.

United States Steel Corporation and Marathon Oil Company: prospectus

Offer to Purchase for Cash
30,000,000 Common Shares
of
MARATHON OIL COMPANY
at
$125 Per Share Net
by
USS, INC.
An Indirect Wholly Owned Subsidiary of
UNITED STATES STEEL CORPORATION

THE PRORATION DATE IS 12:00 MIDNIGHT, NEW YORK CITY TIME, ON SATURDAY, NOVEMBER 28, 1981. THE WITHDRAWAL DEADLINE IS 12:00 MIDNIGHT, NEW YORK CITY TIME, ON THURSDAY, DECEMBER 10, 1981. THE OFFER WILL EXPIRE AT 12:00 MIDNIGHT, NEW YORK CITY TIME, ON THURSDAY, DECEMBER 17, 1981, UNLESS EXTENDED.

IMPORTANT

Any shareholder desiring to tender all or any portion of his Shares should either (1) complete and sign the Letter of Transmittal or a facsimile thereof in accordance with the instructions in the Letter of Transmittal and mail or deliver it with his stock certificate(s) and any other required documents to the Depositary or (2) request his broker, dealer, commercial bank, trust company or other nominee to effect the transaction for him. Shareholders having Shares registered in the name of a broker, dealer, commercial bank, trust company or other nominee must contact such broker, dealer, commercial bank, trust company or other nominee if they desire to tender their Shares.

Questions and requests for assistance or for additional copies of the Offer to Purchase and the Letter of Transmittal may be directed to Georgeson & Co. Inc. (the Information Agent) or to the Dealer Managers. Their telephone numbers are listed at the end of this Offer to Purchase.

The Dealer Managers for the Offer are:
GOLDMAN, SACHS & CO.

November 19, 1981

To the Holders of Common Shares of
MARATHON OIL COMPANY:

USS, Inc., an Ohio corporation (the "Purchaser"), hereby offers to purchase 30,000,000 Common Shares, without par value (the shares subject to the Offer, as well as all other Common Shares, being hereinafter called the "Shares"), of Marathon Oil Company, an Ohio corporation (the "Company"), at $125 per share net to the seller in cash, upon the terms and subject to the conditions set forth in this Offer to Purchase and in the related Letter of Transmittal (which together constitute the "Offer"). The Purchaser is an indirect wholly owned subsidiary of United States Steel Corporation, a Delaware corporation ("United States Steel"). Tendering shareholders will not be obligated to pay brokerage commissions or, except as set forth in Instruction 7 of the Letter of Transmittal, transfer taxes on the purchase of Shares by the Purchaser.

The Company has announced a quarterly dividend of $0.50 per Share, payable on December 10, 1981, to shareholders of record as of November 16, 1981. Shareholders of record on November 16, 1981, will be entitled to such quarterly dividend whether or not they tender their Shares pursuant to the Offer.

The Purchaser's obligation to purchase Shares pursuant to the Offer is conditioned, among other things, upon a minimum of 30,000,000 Shares being properly tendered and not withdrawn prior to the expiration of the Offer. The Purchaser reserves the right, however, to waive such condition. See Section 14 for a discussion of other conditions to the Offer.

The Company has advised the Purchaser that as of November 17, 1981, 58,685,906 Shares were outstanding and an additional 1,317,300 Shares were subject to options issued in connection with various employee benefit plans. Based upon those reported numbers, following the purchase of 30,000,000 Shares pursuant to the Offer, the Purchaser would own approximately 50% of the aggregate of the Shares outstanding and the Shares subject to issuance in connection with such options.

On November 18, 1981, United States Steel, the Purchaser and the Company entered into an Agreement of Merger (the "Merger Agreement") pursuant to which the Purchaser will be merged into the Company (the "Merger") and the Company will thereby become a wholly owned subsidiary of United States Steel. The Merger Agreement provides that the Offer will be the first step in United States Steel's proposed acquisition of the entire equity interest in the Company. Following completion of the Offer, the Merger will be submitted for the approval of the shareholders of the Company. In the Merger, each outstanding Share (other than any Shares that are held by the Company as treasury shares or owned by United States Steel, the Purchaser or any other subsidiary of United States Steel or that are the subject of dissenters' rights, if any have been properly exercised) will be converted into the right to receive $100 principal amount of 12-year 12½% Senior Notes (the "Notes") of United States Steel. See Section 11 for a more detailed description of the Merger and the Notes.

The Company's Board of Directors has unanimously determined that the Offer and the Merger are fair to the shareholders of the Company, has consented to and approved the making of the Offer, and recommends acceptance of the Offer by shareholders of the Company.

The Company has granted to the Purchaser options to purchase (a) up to

10,000,000 Shares at a price of $90 per Share and (b) all rights of the Company in and to certain oil and gas interests and properties included within the Yates Field, Pecos and Crockett Counties, Texas, and related interests, at a price of $2.8 billion. See Section 11.

Pursuant to an Offer to Purchase dated October 30, 1981, as supplemented on November 10, 1981, Mobil Corporation ("Mobil") is offering to purchase for cash up to 40,000,000 Shares at $85 per Share net to the seller (the "Mobil Offer"). The Mobil Offer is conditioned on at least 30,000,000 Shares being properly tendered and not withdrawn at the expiration date thereof. The proration date for the Mobil Offer is 12:00 Midnight, New York City time, on Saturday, November 21, 1981, and the Mobil Offer is scheduled to expire at 12:00 Midnight, New York City time, on Friday, December 11, 1981, unless extended.

As a result of the commencement of this Offer, Shares that have been tendered pursuant to the Mobil Offer may be withdrawn until 12:00 Midnight, New York City time, on Friday, December 4, 1981, if the applicable procedures set forth in Section 3 of the Mobil Offer to Purchase are followed, and until such time may not be accepted for payment by Mobil. Shareholders who desire assistance in withdrawing Shares tendered pursuant to the Mobil Offer may contact the Information Agent at any of the addresses and telephone numbers set forth on the back page of this Offer to Purchase.

On November 1, 1981, the Company instituted an action captioned *Marathon Oil Company* v. *Mobil Oil Corporation and Mobil Oil Corporation and Merrill Lynch, Pierce, Fenner & Smith Incorporated* in the United States District Court for the Northern District of Ohio. The complaint alleges, *inter alia*, that the effect of the proposed acquisition of the Company by Mobil may be substantially to lessen competition or to tend to create a monopoly in violation of Section 7 of the Clayton Act. On November 1, 1981, the United States District Court for the Northern District of Ohio issued an order temporarily restraining Mobil and Merrill Lynch, Pierce, Fenner & Smith Incorporated from taking any further action to implement the Mobil Offer. That order was modified on November 10, 1981, to permit Mobil to continue with the Mobil Offer, provided that Mobil is not permitted to purchase Shares until after the Court rules on the Company's motion for a preliminary injunction. On November 17, 1981, the District Court commenced a hearing to determine whether the Mobil Offer should be preliminarily enjoined. Shareholders of the Company are urged to consult the financial press for further information regarding the Mobil Offer.

The Board of Directors of the Company has determined that the Mobil Offer is grossly inadequate and not in the best interests of the Company or its shareholders and has strongly recommended that the Company's shareholders not tender any Shares in response to the Mobil Offer. See Section 10.

Appendix A | 205

Peavey Company and ConAgra:
joint proxy and prospectus; price information

THE MERGER

The Parties

Peavey. Peavey is a grain merchandiser, an operator of specialty retail stores and a food processor. See "BUSINESS AND PROPERTIES OF PEAVEY".

ConAgra. ConAgra is a basic food business which operates in three industry segments: agriculture, grain and food. See "BUSINESS AND PROPERTIES OF CONAGRA".

Sub. Sub is a wholly owned subsidiary of ConAgra formed for the purpose of the Merger.

Merger Terms

In the Merger, Peavey will be merged into Sub which will be the surviving corporation and change its name to "Peavey Company". Each share of Peavey Common Stock outstanding at the effective time of the Merger (the "Effective Time") (except shares of Peavey Common Stock issued and held in the treasury of Peavey or beneficially owned by ConAgra or Sub or with respect to which dissenters' rights are sought pursuant to Sections 301.40 and 301.44 of the Minnesota Business Corporation Act) shall, at the election of the shareholders subject to the limitations described below, be converted into and exchanged for either (i) a package of .172 shares of ConAgra $2.50 Cumulative Convertible Preferred Stock plus the number of shares of ConAgra Common Stock (computed to four decimal places and rounded up or down to the nearest one thousandth of a share) which is determined by dividing $25.70 by the average of the daily high and low sales prices of ConAgra Common Stock on the New York Stock Exchange-Composite Transactions Tape (the "NYSE-Composite Tape") as reported by *The Wall Street Journal* on the fifteen trading days commencing May 27, 1982 and ending on June 17, 1982 (the "Base Period Stock Price") (a "Stock Election") or (ii) $30.00 in cash (a "Cash Election"). In no event will less than 1.035 shares of ConAgra Common Stock or more than 1.215 shares of ConAgra Common Stock (subject to adjustment for any stock split, reverse stock split or stock dividend with respect to ConAgra Common Stock prior to the Effective Time) be received upon the conversion of any share of Peavey Common Stock which is the subject of a Stock Election. **If a shareholder does not make an effective election, such shareholder will be deemed, subject to the limitations on elections described below, to have made a Stock Election.** The Reorganization Agreement and the Merger Agreement provide that if the aggregate number of shares of Peavey Common Stock as to which Cash Elections are effective exceeds 30% of the issued and outstanding shares of Peavey Common Stock as of the date of the Peavey Shareholders Meeting (the "Cash Election Limitation"), Cash Elections will be eliminated by lot, so as to reduce the number of shares of Peavey Common Stock subject to Cash Elections to a number approximately equal to that permitted by the Cash Election Limitation. Furthermore, if the aggregate number of shares of Peavey Common Stock as to which Stock Elections have effectively been made or which are deemed to be Stock Elections exceeds 70% of the issued and outstanding shares of Peavey Common Stock as of the date of the Peavey Shareholders Meeting (the "Stock Election Limitation"), Stock Elections will be eliminated by lot so as to reduce the number of shares of Peavey Common Stock subject to Stock Elections to a number approximately equal to the Stock Election Limitation. Approximately 6.6% of the outstanding shares of Peavey Common Stock are held by the Trustee of the PS and I Plan (the "Trustee") on behalf of the participants in such plan. The Trustee will make a single Cash Election or Stock Election with respect to all shares of Peavey Common Stock in the PS and I Plan. In light of the purpose of the PS and I Plan, in the event the Stock Election Limitation is exceeded, ConAgra presently intends to instruct the Exchange Agent not to eliminate a Stock Election made by the Trustee in the event that such election is drawn by lot in accordance with the procedures described above. See "Shareholder Elections" in this Summary for information on the procedures for making elections. For more detailed information, see "THE MERGER—Basis for Converting Shares"; "— Shareholder Elections". For information with respect to the participation by Peavey management, and Peavey employees generally, in the PS and I Plan, see "MANAGEMENT OF PEAVEY—Directors"; "—Certain Information Concerning the Board of Directors".

It is intended that the package of ConAgra Common Stock and ConAgra $2.50 Cumulative Convertible Preferred Stock to be exchanged for each share of Peavey Common Stock should have a market value approximately equal to $30.00. It should be recognized, however, that the ConAgra $2.50 Cumulative Convertible Preferred Stock will be newly issued in the Merger and that the market value of the ConAgra securities to be exchanged for each share of Peavey Common Stock in the Merger, at any given time, may be more or less than $30.00 depending on market prices.

(iii)

Appendix B:
Outline of
Basic Tax Laws

For the reader interested in the seemingly endless detail of the tax laws, I have prepared with the help of Oppenheim, Appel, Dixon and Company, in New York City, a summary outline of the basic subjects discussed throughout the book. Citations to the Internal Revenue Code (IRC) and specific legal cases are made. The late Arthur Dixon, managing partner of Oppenheim, Appel, Dixon and Company and former head of the American Institute of Certified Public Accountants, was of great help in putting together this information. He was generally regarded as the most knowledgeable authority in arbitrage tax law.

    I. Reorganizations—general rules.
        1) There are seven defined corporate adjustments which fall within the definition of "reorganization" (IRC Sec. 368(a)(1)).
        A) Type A: statutory merger or consolidation.
        B) Type B: acquisition of stock of one corporation in exchange *solely* for part or all of the voting stock of either the acquiring corporation or its

parent. Acquiring corporation must have "control" (IRC Sec. 368(c)) of acquired corporation immediately after acquisition (whether or not it had such control before the acquisition).

C) Type C: an acquisition by one corporation of substantially all the properties of another corporation, in exchange solely for voting stock of the acquiring corporation or its parent, or in exchange for such voting stock and a limited amount of money or other property, provided the acquired corporation distributes all of the assets, including consideration received from the acquiring corporation and any retained assets, pursuant to the plan of reorganization.

D) Type D: transfer by a corporation of all or part of its assets to a corporation controlled (immediately after the transfer) by the transferor or its shareholders, but only if stock or securities of the controlled corporation are distributed under a plan of reorganization qualifying under IRC Sec. 354, 355 or 356.

E) Type E: recapitalization.

F) Type F: change in identity, form or place of organization.

G) Type G: insolvency reorganization.

II. Statutory mergers and consolidations (Type A) (IRC Sec. 368(a)(1)(B)).

1) Must be a merger or consolidation effected pursuant to the corporation laws of the United States, a state, a territory of the United States, or the District of Columbia.

2) Merger: one corporation absorbs the corporate enterprise of another corporation, with acquiring

corporation stepping into shoes of acquired corporation.
3) Consolidation: combination of two or more corporations into newly formed entity.
4) Transferor corporation or corporations disappear as legal entities.
5) Imposes little or no restrictions on the type of consideration to be used.
   A) Must meet business purposes and continuity of enterprise tests.
   B) Must also satisfy "continuity of interest" test.
      a) Rev. Proc. 77–37, 1977–2 C.B. 568 under IRS guidelines, 50 percent of the value of acquired corporation must be received in form of equity in acquiring corporation by former shareholders.
      b) Courts have permitted lower percentage.
   C) Step-transaction doctrine—various steps leading up to and following exchanges of stock and assets considered in determining whether there is reorganization.
6) Basis of stock and securities received ("nonrecognition property").
   A) Same as basis of property transferred.
      a) Decreased by fair-market value (FMV) of property other than nonrecognition property (including money) received (boot) and by the amount of loss, if any, recognized on exchange.
      b) Increased by "dividends," if any, and amount of gain recognized, if any, on exchange (IRC Sec. 358).
7) Basis of boot (except money) is fair-market value.

8) Holding period of the stock and securities exchanged is "tacked on" to the holding period of the stock and securities received (IRC Sec. 1223(1)).

   A) If debt obligations received are not securities but boot, holding period begins from date of acquisition.

   B) Whether debt obligations are securities depends on such factors as maturity date, degree of participation, and continuing interest in corporation.

      a) Generally, five years' or less term indebtedness is not "security."

      b) Ten years' or more term indebtedness generally is "security."

9) Forward triangular merger (IRC Sec. 368(a)(2)(D)).

   A) Involves target company, a controlled subsidiary, and the parent of the controlled subsidiary.

   B) Target company merges directly into controlled subsidiary and stock of parent company given as consideration for acquisition.

   C) No stock of controlled subsidiary can be given as consideration.

   D) "Substantially all" the properties of the target company must be acquired by controlled subsidiary.

   E) Otherwise, Type A reorganization tests must be satisfied.

10) Reverse triangular merger (IRC Sec. 368(a)(2)(E)).

   A) Controlled subsidiary merges into target company (which is surviving company in the merger).

   B) Shareholders of target company exchange their stock for stock of parent company.

    C) Surviving company must hold "substantially all" of properties of target and subsidiary after transaction.

    D) Former shareholders of target company must exchange, in the transaction, stock constituting "control" of the target company for voting stock of the parent company.

11) Merger combined with a distribution of stock and securities (IRC Sec. 355).

    A) In preparation for a merger, one corporation may have to dispose of a separable business (other corporation does not want it) and transfer business to a newly created corporation.

    B) Shareholders receive stock of unwanted business. It may be tax-free distribution or taxable dividend, depending on satisfaction of IRC Sec. 355 requirements.

    C) Remaining assets merged and may qualify under Type A reorganization (*Commissioner* v. *Mary Archer W. Morris Trust*, 367 F.2d 794 (4th Cir. 1966), *acq.* Rev. Rul. 68–603, 1968–2 C.B. 148).

III. Acquisitions of stock for voting stock (Type B) (IRC Sec. 368 (a)(1)(B)).

1) Acquisition solely for part or all of voting stock (common or preferred) of either:

    A) Acquiring corporation;

    B) Corporation in control of the acquiring corporation.

2) No boot.

3) Acquiring corporation must be in "control" of the acquired corporation immediately after the acquisition.

    A) Control is defined as ownership of stock possessing at least 80 percent of total combined voting power of all classes of stock entitled to vote, plus

    B) At least 80 percent of the total number of shares of all other classes of stock.

4) Solely for voting stock requirement.

    A) Strict rule.

        a) Warrants to purchase voting stock in acquiring corporation will not qualify (*Southwest Consol. Corp.*, 315 U.S. 194 (1942)).

        b) Convertible voting preferred with rights does not qualify (Rev. Rul. 70–108, 1970–1 C.B. 78).

    B) A valid Type B reorganization will not be destroyed because debenture holders of acquired corporation receive *debentures* of acquiring corporation (payment not made directly or indirectly for acquired corporation's stock), even if held predominantly by nonshareholder creditors (Rev. Rul. 69–142, 1969–1 C.B. 107).

    C) Payment of regular (and under certain circumstances special) dividend contemporaneous with reorganization will not adversely affect "solely for voting stock" requirement if funds not supplied directly or indirectly by acquiring corporation (Rev. Rul. 69–443, 1969–2 C.B. 54 and Rev. Rul. 70–172, 1970–1 C.B. 77).

5) Effects of Type B reorganization.

    A) Since no boot received, no gain or loss recognized to shareholders of acquired corporation.

    B) Tax basis in shares of acquiring corporation is same as basis in acquired corporation shares.

    C) Holding period in shares of acquiring corporation includes holding period in acquired corporation shares.

IV. Acquisitions of property for voting stock (Type C) (IRC Sec. 368 (a)(1)(C)).

  1) Acquisition of "substantially all" assets of another corporation solely for voting stock of acquiring corporation or parent corporation, but not both, if the acquired corporation distributes all its assets, including consideration received from the acquired corporation and any retained assets, pursuant to a plan of reorganization.

    A) Distribution requirement may be waived by regulations, subject to conditions prescribed by IRS.

  2) Qualifying as a Type C reorganization.

    A) Voting stock requirement.

      a) Assumption of liabilities disregarded for "solely" for voting stock purposes and in determining whether transaction qualifies as a reorganization; if only voting stock exchanged, amount of liabilities assumed (or taken "subject to") immaterial (IRC Sec. 368(a)(1)(C) and Sec. 357(a)).

      b) Liabilities may be important in computing boot (IRC Sec. IV(2)(A)(e), below).

      c) Stock of acquiring corporation used in reorganization may qualify under certain circumstances where convertible to stock of corporation's parent (Rev. Rul. 69–265, 1969–1 C.B. 109).

      d) Payment of reorganization expenses of acquired corporation by acquiring corporation will not violate "solely for voting stock" requirement (Rev. Rul. 73–54, 1973–1 C.B. 187).

e) Exception to "solely for voting stock" requirement "boot relaxation rule" (IRC Sec. 368(a)(2)(B)).

  I) Property acquired for voting stock must have value at least equal to 80 percent of FMV of transferor corporation's property (including retained property).

  II) Up to 20 percent of property, by FMV, may be acquired for money or "other property."

  III) For purposes of 20-percent requirement in (II), liabilities assumed (or taken "subject to") by acquiring corporation treated as money, thereby reducing amount of money or other property which can be paid.

  IV) If liabilities of acquired corporation assumed exceed 20 percent of FMV of all property of acquired corporation, any boot will cause transaction to fail to qualify as reorganization.

B) "Substantially all" (90 percent/70 percent) test.

  a) Must look to facts of individual case.

  b) Courts generally apply test to corporation's operating business assets.

  c) IRS ruling position: 90 percent of FMV of the net assets and 70 percent of the FMV of the gross assets must be transferred (Rev. Proc. 77–37, 1977–2 C.B. 568).

  d) Pre–Type C reorganization dividend not within "substantially all" test but if payment of dividend occurs after asset reorganization exchange, both cash to pay dividend and amount of liability for payment taken into account for "substantially all" test (Rev. Rul. 74–457, 1974–2 C.B. 122).

V. Receipt of boot in reorganizations (IRC Sec. 356).

1) Money or property other than that which can be received tax-free (IRC Sec. 354, 355).

2) Can include securities.

A) Principal amount of securities received does not exceed principal amount of the securities surrendered—no boot.

B) Principal amount of securities received is greater than amount surrendered—boot to extent of FMV of excess principal amount.

C) Where no securities are surrendered, principal amount of all securities received is boot (IRC Sec. 354(a), Sec. 356(d)).

3) Any loss on an exchange or distribution is not recognized.

4) Status of property as boot.

A) Certificates of contingent interest (Rev. Rul. 57–586, 1957–2 C.B. 249).

B) Stock rights and stock warrants as "other property" (Treas. Reg. Sec. 1.354—1(e) and *William H. Bateman*, 40 T.C. 408 (1963)).

5) Effect of boot.

A) Gain, if any, recognized in an amount not in excess of the boot (IRC Sec. 354 and Sec. 356(a)(1)).

B) Transaction must qualify as reorganization for limitation rule of IRC Sec. 354 and Sec. 356 to apply (*Commissioner* v. *Turnbow*, 368 U.S. 337 (1961)).

C) Taxation of gain.

a) Dividend if exchange "has effect of distribution of a dividend" (taking into account attribution rules); amount of dividend to each distributee is portion of recognized gain not in excess of ratable share of earnings and profits (IRC Sec. 356(a)(2)).

b) Remainder, if any, of gain recognized treated as gain from exchange of property (IRC Sec. 356(a)(2)).

c) Whether exchange has effect of distribution of a dividend tested under redemption principles of IRC Sec. 302 (Rev. Rul. 74–515, 1974–2 C.B. 118; Rev. Rul. 75–83, 1975–1 C.B. 112).

d) Proper application of IRC Sec. 302 analysis to Sec. 356 (a)(2) unresolved.

   I) *Wright* v. *U.S.*, 482 F.2d 600 (8th Cir. 1973): in case involving consolidation of two corporations, with taxpayer having substantial interest in both, distribution treated as hypothetical redemption of *acquiring* corporation stock for boot.

   II) Rev. Rul. 75–83, 1975–1 C.B. 112: distribution treated as having been made by *acquired* corporation; *Wright* expressly not followed.

   III) *Shimberg* v. *U.S.*, 577 F.2d 283 (5th Cir. 1978): distribution treated as having been made by acquired corporation; treatment of distribution as if no reorganization had taken place or as if distribution made before reorganization.

VI. Interrelationship of reorganization sections.

1) Type B reorganization followed by an IRC Sec. 332 liquidation treated as part of single plan will be considered a Type C reorganization (Treas. Reg. Sec. 1.382(b)—1(a)(6), Rev. Rul. 67–274, 1967–2 C.B. 141).

VII. Liquidations.

  1) Complete liquidations (IRC Sec. 331(a)(1), Sec. 346(a)).

    A) Amounts distributed in complete liquidation of a corporation are full payment in *exchange* for the shareholder's stock.

    B) Includes first distribution of a series of distributions in redemption of stock pursuant to a plan.

    C) If stock is a "capital asset" in hands of shareholder, a complete liquidation would produce capital gains or losses.

      a) Dealer must designate the stock as held for investment before close of day of acquisition and not hold stock primarily for sale to customers in ordinary course of trade or business at any time thereafter to receive capital gain treatment (IRC Sec. 1236 (a)(1), (2)).

    D) Gain or loss upon liquidation is the difference between the adjusted basis of shareholder's stock and the FMV of the liquidating distribution (IRC Sec. 1001(A)).

  2) Partial liquidations.

    A) Applicable only to noncorporate shareholders (IRC Sec. 302 (e)).

    B) Distribution not essentially equivalent to a dividend (determined at corporate level rather than shareholder level) pursuant to plan; occurs within taxable year in which plan is adopted or within succeeding taxable year (IRC Sec. 302 (b)(4), Sec. 302 (e)).

    a) "Termination of business": partial liquidation includes (but not limited to) distribution attributable to corporation's ceasing to conduct, or consists of assets of, a "qualified trade or business"; immediately after distribution, distributing corporation actively engaged in conduct of "qualified trade or business."

    b) "Qualified trade or business": trade or business actively conducted throughout five-year period ending on date of redemption and not acquired by corporation within such period in a taxable (in whole or in part) transaction (IRC Sec. 302 (e), Sec. 302(e)(3)).

    c) Redemption in (a) above may be pro rata with respect to shareholders.

C) Taxation.

    a) If a partial liquidation, treated as exchange for the stock (IRC Sec. 331).

        I) Difference between amount received and basis of stock is capital gain or loss.

        II) If stock is not a capital asset to shareholder then ordinary gain or loss is recognized.

    b) If not qualifying as a partial liquidation, treated like redemption.

        I) Exchange (capital gains on loss of stock are capital asset to shareholder) (IRC Sec. 302(a)), or

        II) Dividends (IRC Sec. 302(d) and 301).

3) Twelve-month liquidation (IRC Sec. 337).

A) Generally, no gain or loss to corporation on sale or exchange of the property after adoption of twelve-month plan of complete liquidation (IRC Sec. 337(a)).
B) Nonqualifying assets and dispositions.
   a) Certain installment obligations and stock in trade and inventory (except in case of bulk sale of substantially all inventory to one person in one transaction) (IRC Sec. 337(b)).
   b) Recapture of depreciation and investment tax credit.
C) Nonqualifying liquidations (IRC Sec. 337(c)).
   a) Liquidation of subsidiary corporations under IRC Sec. 332 (IRC Sec. 337(c)(2)).
   b) Sales or exchanges following the adoption of plan of complete (one-month) liquidation under IRC Sec. 333 (IRC Sec. 337(c)(2)).
   c) Sales or exchanges of shares in "collapsible corporations"—see discussion at subsection (E) below (IRC Sec. 337(c)(1)(A) and Sec. 341).
D) If impossible for corporation to distribute all assets within twelve-month period, final liquidating distribution often in form of units of beneficial interest in liquidating trust.
   a) Considered "grantor trust."
   b) Unit holders treated as having realized proportionate share of each item of income, gain, and expense.
   c) Unit holder's holding period in trust unit and assets begins with date of distribution of trust unit (Rev. Rul. 72–137, 1971–1 C.B. 100).
E) "Collapsible corporation" (IRC Sec. 341).

a) Definition: corporation formed or availed of principally for manufacture, construction, or production of property, or for the purchase of "Section 341 assets," or to hold stock in a corporation so formed or availed of with a view to:

    I) A sale or exchange of stock by shareholders or distribution to them before corporation realizes two thirds of taxable income to be derived from property and

    II) Realization by shareholders of gain attributable to such property (IRC Scc. 341(b)(1)).

b) "Section 341 assets."

    I) Inventory, stock in trade, property held primarily for sale to customers, certain unrealized receivables, and certain real property and depreciable property used in trade or business and

    II) Held for less than three years (IRC Sec. 342(b)(3)).

c) Corporation may be treated as collapsible if manufacture, construction, or production is principal corporate activity, even if "view to" collapse not principal corporate activity when corporation formed or availed of (*Edward Weil*, 28 T.C. 809, *aff'd* 252 F.2d 805 (2d Cir. 1958)).

d) Gain otherwise constituting long-term gain to a shareholder can be taxed at ordinary income rates if it arises from:

    I) Actual sale or exchange of the collapsible corporation's stock.

II) Distributions in complete or partial liquidation of collapsible corporation representing exchange for stock.

III) Distribution by collapsible corporation to extent it exceeds basis of the stock and is treated as a sale or exchange under IRC Sec. 301(c)(3)(A).

VIII. Distributions in redemption of stock (IRC Sec. 302).

1) Redemptions treated as exchanges (capital gains (losses) or ordinary income (losses)).

A) Not essentially equivalent to dividends (IRC Sec. 302(B)(1)).

a) *United States* v. *Davis*, 397 U.S. 30 (1970): redemption must result in meaningful reduction of shareholder's proportionate interest in corporation; attribution rules apply.

b) Rev. Rul. 75–502, 1975–2 C.B. 111: decreased ownership from 57 percent to 50 percent, other 50 percent held by single unrelated party; redemption not essentially equivalent to dividend.

c) Rev. Rul. 76–364, 1976–2 C.B. 91: decrease in ownership from 27 percent to 22 percent, no longer able to control with two other parties; meaningful reduction, redemption not essentially equivalent to dividend.

d) Rev. Rul. 81–289, 1981–2 C.B. 82: shareholder owning less than 1 percent of publicly traded corporation's outstanding stock has portion of stock redeemed pursuant to tender offer that also reduces number of shares held by other shareholders. Pro rata stock interest not reduced. Redemption does

not reduce shareholder's right to vote, participate in current earnings, and accumu-
late surplus or share in corporation's net
assets on liquidation. IRS held redemption
is not meaningful reduction and is not exchanged under IRC Sec. 302 (b)(1).

B) Substantially disproportionate redemption of
stock (IRC Sec. 302(b)(2)).

a) Less than 50 percent of total combined voting power of all classes of stock entitled to
vote after redemption (IRC Sec. 302(b)(2)(B)).

b) Holdings of shareholder after the redemption are less than 80 percent of the voting
power held prior to the redemption (IRC
Sec. 302(b)(2)(C)).

c) Shareholder's ownership of common stock
(whether voting or nonvoting) before and
after redemption meets 80-percent test (IRC
Sec. 302(b)(2)(C)).

d) Tests applied to each shareholder separately (Treas. Reg. Sec. 1.302–3).

e) Attribution rules apply (see discussion at
(C)(b), below).

C) Termination of shareholder's interest (IRC Sec.
302(b)(3)).

a) Shareholder must completely terminate
proprietary interest in corporation though
can retain or acquire other interest in corporation:

I) As landlord, provided that rent not dependent on future earnings or subor-
dinate to personal creditors (Rev. Rul.
70–639, 1970–2 C.B. 74; Rev. Rul. 77–
467, 1977–2 C.B. 92; and Treas. Reg.
Sec. 1.302–4(D)).

II) As officer and director (Rev. Rul. 76–
524, 1976–2 C.B. 94).

III) Credit redemptions are tolerated except where the "debt" represents continued equity interest; Internal
Revenue Service refuses to rule on extended payments where amount is
based on or contingent on future earnings, maintenance of working capital
at a certain level (Rev. Proc. 80–22,
1980–1 C.B. 654).

b) Constructive ownership of stock (IRC Sec.
318).

I) A taxpayer is considered as owning any
stock which is owned by certain family members, partnerships, estates,
certain trusts, or subject to option held
by him. Subject to certain limitations,
entities in which taxpayer beneficially has interest treated as owning
stock owned directly by him.

II) Individual deemed to own stock owned
by spouse (other than spouse legally
separated under decree of separate
maintenance), children, grandchil-
dren, and parents (IRC Sec. 318
(a)(1)(A)).

III) No attribution between brother and
sister (IRC Sec. 318 (a)(1)(A)).

IV) Stock owned by a corporation is at-
tributed pro rata to those shareholders
(if any) who own 50 percent or more
by value of its stock (IRC Sec. 318
(a)(2)(C)).

V) Attribution of stock to or from S Corporation and shareholders applied in same manner as if S Corporation (and shareholders) were a partnership (with partners) (IRC Sec. 318(a)(5)(E)).

c) Family attribution may be waived in certain circumstances (IRC Sec. 302(c)(2)).

2) Redemptions treated as dividends.

A) When subsection (1) above does not apply.

B) Dividends can be fully or partially taxable (IRC Sec. 301).

C) Dividends-received deductions, for corporations.

a) Generally a deduction from taxable income of 85 percent of dividends received from domestic corporations (IRC Sec. 243 (a)(1)).

b) Limitations on aggregate amount of deduction (IRC Sec. 246(c)(1)(A), (B), Sec. 246(c)(3)).

I) No reduction unless corporation has more than forty-five days of good holding period by close of forty-fifth day after ex-dividend date.

II) No deduction to extent the taxpayer is under obligation (short sale or otherwise) to make corresponding payments with respect to substantially identical stock or securities.

III) Ninety-day holding period rule applies in the case of certain preference dividends where dividends attributable to period or periods aggregate in excess of 366 days (IRC Sec. 246(c)(2)).

c) Determination of holding period (IRC Sec. 246(c)(3), 246(c)(4)).
   I) Includes day of disposition, not day of acquisition.
   II) Days following forty-fifth day after ex-dividend date not counted.
   III) Days on which taxpayer holds a put, is under a contractual obligation to sell or has made (and not closed) a short sale of substantially identical stock, or writes a call that is not a "qualified covered call" do not count as good holding-period days.
   IV) Days on which taxpayer has diminished his risk of loss by holding one or more other positions with respect to "substantially similar or related property" (to be defined in regulations) also do not count as good holding-period days.
d) "Qualified covered call."
   I) Exchange-traded call option written by taxpayer on stock held by taxpayer (or stock acquired by taxpayer in connection with granting of option) that results in capital-gain or -loss treatment to writer.
   II) Call option granted by options dealer in connection with his activity in dealing in options not qualified.
   III) Call option must have more than thirty days to expiration and a strike price not less than the first available strike below the closing price on the previous day.

IV) Call option must have a strike price no lower than the second available strike below the closing stock price of the previous day in the case of options written with more than ninety days to expiration and with a strike price over $50.

V) A qualified covered call cannot be more than $10 in-the-money if stock price is $150 or less.

VI) Strike price must be at least 85 percent of stock price if closing stock price on previous day is $25 or less.

VII) In all cases, if opening price of stock on day options is written is greater than 110 percent of preceding day's closing price, opening price, rather than preceding day's closing price, is used to determine lowest acceptable strike price for qualified covered call.

e) Debt-financed portfolio stock (IRC Sec. 246(A)).

I) Dividends-received deduction for dividends on debt-financed portfolio stock reduced by amount determined by reference to indebtedness "directly attributable" to purchase or carrying dividend-paying stock.

II) Widely held publicly traded stock generally treated as portfolio stock.

D) "Extraordinary" dividend.

a) Corporate shareholder's basis in stock reduced by nontaxed portion (after taking into account dividends-received deduction) of any nonliquidating "extraordinary" dividend if stock sold or exchanged before it is held more than one year.

b) "Extraordinary" dividends include dividends received within any eighty-five-day period with FMV equal to or greater than 10 percent of shareholder's adjusted basis on stock (5 percent in case of preferred stock).

c) All dividends received on stock having ex-dividend dates during 365-consecutive-day period treated as "extraordinary" if dividends aggregate more than 20 percent of corporate shareholder's basis in stock.

d) Dividends-received deduction holding-period rules generally apply.

IX. Distribution of stock and stock rights (IRC Sec. 305).

1) Generally gross income does not include the amount of any distribution of stock of a corporation made by such corporation to its shareholders with respect to the corporation's stock (IRC Sec. 305(a)).

A) Only pertains to corporation's *own* stock (including rights to acquire such stock).

B) Debt instruments are excluded.

C) Basis.

a) Shareholder must allocate basis of old stock between the old and the new stock (IRC Sec. 307(a)).

b) Basis of dividend stock received on stock purchased at various times and at different prices computed by allocating to each lot of purchased stock the proportionate amount of dividend stock attributable to it (Rev. Rul. 71–350, 1971–2 C.B. 1976).

D) Holding period of new stock includes period of old stock (IRC Sec. 1223 (5)).
E) Earnings and profits.
 a) Distributing corporation does not reduce earnings and profits (IRC Sec. 312(a)(1)(B)).
 b) No increase in a recipient corporation's earnings and profits (IRC Sec. 312(f)(2)).
2) Exceptions to general nonrecognition rule.
 A) Distribution at election of any of shareholders payable either in stock (or rights) of distributing company or property (IRC Sec. 305(b)(1)).
 B) "Disproportionate distribution": distribution (or series of distributions) having result of receipt of property by some shareholders and increase in proportionate interest of other shareholders in assets or earnings and profits of corporation (IRC Sec. 305(b)(2)).
  a) Stock and property distributions need not be pursuant to plan of distributions (Treas. Reg. Sec. 1.305–3(b)(2)).
  b) Presumption of independent transactions if distributions not part of a plan and are separated by more than thirty-six months (Treas. Reg. 1.305–3(b)(4)).
  c) Distribution of property pursuant to isolated redemption (for example, pursuant to tender offer) does not result in "disproportionate distribution," even though IRC Sec. 301 or Sec. 356(a)(2) distribution (Treas. Reg. Sec. 1.305–3(b)(3)).
  d) *"De minimis"* rule does not apply.
  e) Additional shares issued to sellers in connection with tax-free reorganizations if certain contingencies occur.

       I) Literally could be taxable as disproportionate distribution if connected with property distribution.

      II) Implication is they are not: income-tax regulations exempt from taxable dividend provisions adjustments in purchase price to be paid by distributing corporation (Treas. Reg. Sec. 1.305–1(c)).

C) Distribution having result of receipt of preferred stock by some common shareholders and receipt of common stock by other common shareholders (IRC Sec. 305(b)(3)).

D) Distributions on preferred stock (other than increase in conversion ratio of convertible preferred stock made solely to take account of stock dividend or stock split with respect to stock into which convertible stock is convertible) (IRC Sec. 305(b)(4)).

    a) Redemption premium (excess of redemption price over issue price on preferred) does not constitute constructive stock dividend if it constitutes reasonable redemption premium (Treas. Reg. 1.305–5(b)(1)).

    b) Redemption premium is considered reasonable if it is in nature of penalty for premature redemption of preferred stock and if premium does not exceed amount the corporation would be required to pay for right to make such premature redemption under market conditions existing at time of issuance; such amount can be established by comparing call premium rates on comparable stock paying comparable dividends (Treas. Reg. 1.305–5(b)(2)).

    c) Redemption premium not in excess of 10 percent of issue price and not redeemable for five years from date of issue is considered reasonable (Treas. Reg. 1.305–5(b)(2)).

    d) Redemption premium of 10 percent or less on preferred agreed upon merger transaction but exceeded 10 percent later due to market decline was not bargained for, no intent, not deemed excessive (Rev. Rul. 75–468, 1975–2 C.B. 115 and Rev. Rul. 81–190, 1981–2 C.B. 84).

  E) Distributions of convertible preferred stock unless it is established that it will not have disproportionate result (IRC Sec. 305(b)(5)).

  F) Constructive distributions: escalating redemption prices, antidilution clauses, call premiums, recapitalizations (IRC Sec. 305(c)).

3) Treatment of taxable stock dividends.

  A) Treated as a distribution of property discussed at Section X below.

  B) In taxable election distribution (IRC Sec. 305(b)(1)) the amount of the distribution for tax purposes depends upon whether shareholder takes stock or rights of the distributing corporation, or chooses property.

    a) Stock or rights measured by FMV (Treas. Reg. Sec. 1.305–2 and 1.301–1(d)).

    b) Stock or rights holding period commences with date of acquisition (no provision in IRC Sec. 1223).

    c) Earnings and profits reduced by FMV of stock or rights (Treas. Reg. Sec. 1.312–1(d)).

    d) Normal dividend and earnings and profits rules govern tax treatment of property (Treas. Reg. Sec. 1.305–2(b)).

    C) Other taxable distributions under IRC Sec. 305(b) generally have same tax consequences as in taxable election distribution.

4) Acquisitive reorganizations.

    A) Buyer issues stock: beware of taxable stock dividends rules, especially where preferred stock issued.

    B) Taxable dividend rules can override nonrecognition rules unless under IRC Sec. 354.

    C) Receipt of preferred stock in a tax-free reorganization not treated as taxable dividend to which IRC Sec. 301 applies by reason of the application of IRC Sec. 305(b) and 305(c); subsequent changes in redemption price or conversion ratio of preferred stock may result in taxable dividend (Rev. Rul. 82–158, 1982–2 C.B. 77).

X. Distributions of property (IRC Sec. 301).

  1) General rule.

    A) A distribution by a corporation is "dividend" if it is paid out of current or accumulated earnings and profits.

    B) To extent earnings are insufficient, return of capital up to shareholder's adjusted basis.

    C) Excess over basis (and dividend portion) is gain from sale or exchange of property.

  2) Distributions can be in cash or other property.

  3) Amount of distributions to corporate distributees—distributions in kind.

    A) Amount of a distribution to the distributee is the property's FMV, or

    B) Its adjusted basis in the hands of the distributing corporation immediately before distribution (increased by amount of gain, if any, recognized to distributing corporation or distribution),

C) Whichever is the lesser,

D) Reduced, but not below zero, for liabilities assumed (or taken subject to) (IRC Sec. 301(b)).

4) Basis.

A) Noncorporate distributee: FMV.

B) Corporate distributee: FMV, or adjusted basis in hands of distributing corporation immediately before distribution (increased by amount of gain, if any, recognized to distributing corporation on distribution), whichever is the lesser (IRC Sec. 301(d)).

5) Distributing corporation's earnings and profits generally reduced (but not below zero) by amount of money and adjusted basis of distributed property (IRC Sec. 312(a)).

A) Subject to special rules and adjustments.

B) Amount of reduction reduced for liabilities and increased where gain recognized to distributing corporation on distribution (IRC Sec. 312(c) and Treas. Reg. Sec. 1.312–3).

6) Distribution of corporation's own obligations.

A) Evidenced by notes, bonds, debentures or other securities.

B) Amount of distribution and basis to individual distributee is FMV of obligation (IRC Sec. 301(b)(1)(A) and IRC Sec. 301(d)(1)).

C) Amount of distribution and basis to corporate distributee is generally lesser of FMV or adjusted basis in hands of distributing corporation immediately before distribution (IRC Sec. 301(b)(1)(B), IRC Sec. 301(d)(2), and Treas. Reg. Sec. 1.301–1(d)).

D) Distributing corporation's earnings and profits reduced by principal amount of obligation (or issue price in case of original issue discount obligation) (IRC Sec. 312(a)(2)).

7) Distributions of appreciated property to corporate shareholders.

A) Gain (but not loss) generally recognized to distributing corporation on ordinary nonliquidating distribution of appreciated property (other than distribution of corporation's own obligations), whether or not it qualifies as dividend, as if property sold for FMV (IRC Sec. 311(d)).

B) Corporate shareholder's holding period for appreciated property distributed by another corporation generally begins on date of distribution, subject to exemptions (IRC Sec. 301(e)(1)).

XI. Step transactions.

1) Corporation may tender shares of target company for cash up to 50 percent and then exchange remaining shares of target company for its own stock.

2) Although this can qualify for a valid Type B reorganization (Section III above) the problem for the former shareholders lies in the treatment of the tender as part of (or a step in) the merger or a wholly separate transaction.

A) If the cash tender is considered a step in the merger transaction, then it is boot, taxable as a dividend or as gain from exchange of property (Section V above).

B) If the cash tender is considered a separate transaction, then the cash will be considered an "exchange," thus providing the capital gains (or loss).

3) Determination of status.

A) "Old and cold" or part of unitary plan, time may not be a factor.
B) Intent and interdependence.
C) Some courts have looked to a "binding commitment" (*Commissioner* v. *Gordon*, 391 U.S. 83(1968)) but this case may only be an aid to taxpayers wishing to invoke the doctrine.

Index

235